THE BATTLE OF GUILFORD COURTHOUSE

THE BATTLE
OF GUILFORD
COURTHOUSE

A Most Desperate Engagement

JOHN R. MAASS

THE
History
PRESS

Published by The History Press
Charleston, SC
www.historypress.com

Copyright © 2020 by John R. Maass
All rights reserved

Front cover image courtesy of White Historic Art.

First published 2020

ISBN 9781467139120

Library of Congress Control Number: 2019954281

This book is dedicated to the Washington and Lee University class of 1987, of which the author is a proud member.

Non incautus futuri.

CONTENTS

CONTENTS

ACKNOWLEDGEMENTS

A book is not produced by the author alone. Many generous people and organizations helped me research and write this book over the past few years, and I wish to express my sincere thanks to them. These include Charles Baxley, Jim Piecuch, Cheryl Bratten, Joshua Howard, Paul Morando, Robert Orrison, James Tobias, Erik Goldstein, John Durham, Scott Douglas, Mark Bradley, Jay Callaham, Glenn Williams, Patrick Jennings, Todd Braisted, John Beakes, Jeff Lambert, Ellen Clark, the Southern Campaigns of the American Revolution, the U.S. Army Center of Military History, the National Museum of the U.S. Army, Guilford Courthouse National Military Park, and the Society of the Cincinnati (Anderson House).

I wish to express particular appreciation to Jeff and Amy Oves of Kernersville, North Carolina, for graciously hosting me for a weekend while I took photographs for the book and visited obscure historical sites, and to Barbara Bass of South Boston, Virginia, for leading me on a tour of The Prizery exhibits and the site of Boyd's Ferry on the Dan River.

INTRODUCTION

Let me still hear the Cannons thundering Voice,
In terror then run; that sweet noise
Rings in my ears more pleasing than the sound
Of any music consort that can be found…
Then to see legs and arms torn ragged fly
And bodies gasping all dismembered lie.
—George Lauder, "The Scottish Soldier," 1629

In the thinly settled North Carolina Piedmont, a rough highway known as the "Great Salisbury Road" led late eighteenth-century travelers westward from Hillsborough on to the crossroads village of Salisbury on the Yadkin River, ninety miles away through a rolling, thickly wooded country with few towns, scattered farms, and numerous creeks and rivers. One of the small rustic villages along this well-used sandy road was Guilford Courthouse, the judicial seat of the backcountry county of Guilford, recently formed in 1771. A small log or wooden frame courthouse and a tiny jail were erected there in 1774, at the junction with Reedy Fork Road, which led northward.

Around Guilford Courthouse in the late winter of 1781, the quiet forests of the hilly sylvan countryside, populated in part by peaceful Quakers as early as the 1750s, were suddenly shattered by the booming thunder of cannon fire, musket volleys blasting in the bare woods, and the anguished shouts and cries of thousands of men in two weary armies aiming to destroy one another. This violent clash was fought on a cold, wet afternoon on

March 15, during which American forces under Major General Nathanael Greene engaged Lieutenant General Charles, Lord Cornwallis's British army in a bitter two-hour contest that was, in Greene's poignant words, "long, obstinate, and bloody."

The frightful contest at Guilford was "a severe conflict" and produced heavy casualties. The troops made repeated use of their flintlock muskets, steel bayonets, and dragoon swords in hand-to-hand fighting, which killed and wounded about eight hundred men. Some soldiers fled the field in terror, while others played dead on the ground to avoid capture. Several participants in the grueling battle wrote that for much of the ferocious contest, it was long in doubt which side would emerge the victor, so fierce was the struggle. In the end, however, a cautious General Greene withdrew his battalions from the battleground, letting Lord Cornwallis claim a victory. "Except [for] the honor of the field[,] they have nothing to boast of," Greene said.[1]

It soon became painfully obvious that the British triumph was pyrrhic. Hundreds of redcoats lay dead and wounded in the damp fields and forests, while the rest of the king's troops were too drained to pursue the rebels with any strength as a steady drizzle began to fall. After two days, the Americans saw the odd circumstance of a triumphant enemy general marching his men away from the site of his bloody victory, limping toward the far-off Carolina coast and giving up the fruits of hard-fought operations. It would not be the last time Greene and his army would miss out on a victory on the battlefield or siege lines but emerge the victors nonetheless.

The campaign leading up to the Battle of Guilford Courthouse was strenuous, dramatic, and long in doubt. While Greene's army could not claim a triumph after "the Guilford battle," as many veterans and civilians later called it, two and a half years later they watched British forces evacuate their long-held garrisons in the South after American independence was secured. As it turned out, the ferocious battle that raged around the little courthouse hamlet in North Carolina that winter day was one of the most critical factors in securing that liberty in the newly created United States.

Prologue

"The Highest Honor to Yourself"

The South Gets a Yankee General

*I only lament that my abilities are not more competent
to the duties that will be required of me.*
—*Major General Nathanael Greene, October 1780*

In the early fall of 1780, the American Revolution seemed to be at a low point for the Patriots. General George Washington, the Continental Army's commander-in-chief since 1775, found himself and the cause of independence in a whirlwind of danger and conspiracy. One of his most capable and trusted subordinates, the mercurial Major General Benedict Arnold, had just been unmasked as a traitor after trying to "give over" the key American defensive post at West Point on the Hudson River in New York to the British in September. Moreover, after his abortive attempt at treachery, Arnold fled to an enemy ship anchored in the river, a deceitful act that left Washington enraged and astonished. It was, Washington wrote, "a scene of treason as shocking as it was unexpected." The American commander also feared that "the enemy may have it in contemplation to attempt some enterprise" against the run-down defenses at West Point, and he worked feverishly to secure the post from potential British attacks.[2]

As part of Washington's effort to hold the vital Hudson River defenses during the chaotic scene after Arnold's duplicity, he appointed thirty-eight-year-old Major General Nathanael Greene as commander at West Point and ordered him on October 6, 1780, to bring two divisions of Continental

West Point on the Hudson River, scene of Arnold's treason in 1780. *Library of Congress.*

soldiers there. Greene, having long desired this assignment, gave orders the next day for his troops to move northward from their camps at Haverstraw, New York, on the west bank of the Hudson, about thirty-five miles north of New York City. When Greene and his soldiers arrived at West Point, they found the fortifications in "a miserable situation" and the defenders woefully short on food and forage. The deplorable state of the earthworks and the garrison resulted from Arnold's neglect, part of his secret plan to allow the British to take the post.[3]

Only one week after assuming command at West Point, however, Greene received new orders from General Washington, who was at the main Continental Army camps at Passaic Falls, New Jersey, a day's march from enemy-held New York. In an October 14 letter sent by an express courier, Washington appointed Greene "Commander of the Southern Army," which was then in the Carolinas facing a powerful British threat led by Lieutenant General Charles, 2nd Earl Cornwallis. "As Congress have been pleased to leave the officer to command on this occasion to my choice," Washington explained, "it is my wish to appoint you." Greene read that he was expected to leave for the South "as soon as circumstances will possibly admit." Washington ended his letter to Greene with an expression of great confidence. "I have only to add," he concluded, "that

Engrav'd for the Columbian Magazine

MAJ.ᴿ GEN.ᴸ GREENE.

Early depiction of General Greene, 1780s. *Library of Congress.*

I wish your earliest arrival, that there be no circumstances to retard your proceeding to the southward, and that the command may be attended with the most interesting good consequences to the States, and the highest honor to yourself."[4]

Greene could not have been surprised by his new assignment to replace Major General Horatio Gates, then the Southern Department commander. Gates's mixed force of Continental regulars and southern militia regiments suffered an overwhelming defeat against Cornwallis's British army several miles north of Camden, South Carolina, on August 16, 1780. Consequently, that fall Congress authorized Washington to choose Gates's successor in the aftermath of the Patriot debacle.[5]

Rumors had come to Greene in September that he might be chosen as the new American commander in the South. Still, Greene had suspected that another general would receive the appointment, since he had just taken up his new assignment at West Point. "Being fixed here" on the Hudson, "it will be difficult for the General [Washington] to call me away immediately," Greene believed, just one day before he received his new orders. Greene had even thought that Gates might retain his command in the South, and thus he sent for his wife, Catherine, in Rhode Island to join him for the winter.[6]

Greene showed no hesitation accepting the new southern assignment. He had received Washington's orders on the night of the fifteenth and replied the next day. He was grateful for the opportunity to have an independent command, having been an indispensable subordinate since 1775 and, until recently, the American army's most proficient quartermaster general for almost three years. "I am fully sensible of the honor you do me," he wrote to his commander, "and will endeavor to manifest my gratitude by a conduct that will not disgrace the appointment." He added that he hoped "my country will have little cause to complain" about the "zeal and attention" he would bring to his new command.[7]

Greene also wrote to his wife that day. He tried to console Catherine, whom he knew would be greatly disappointed at his new, distant post, but he was not entirely truthful about his ambitions and satisfaction at having received the southern command. The general wrote of his dread at getting the orders, which were "so foreign from my wishes that I am distressed exceedingly." He had been looking forward to spending the winter months with her at West Point, he told her, but it was now not meant to be. "How unfriendly is war to domestic happiness," Greene wrote. He also was concerned that her fragile health might be further endangered by a southern relocation. "Poor girl," he wrote to a fellow officer, "it will prove almost fatal to her" if she accompanied him to the Carolinas. Although he asked Washington's permission to return to his home in Rhode Island for several days to see his wife, attend to his personal and financial affairs there, and pack for his long journey to the South, Washington did not allow it; Greene was thus obliged to leave quickly from his riverside headquarters. "God bless you my love and support your spirits," he concluded in his letter to Catherine.[8]

Contrary to these sentiments expressed to his wife, Greene had long coveted such an independent command. In fact, far back in 1778, Greene had told Washington that he would be "happy" to lead American forces in the South.[9] As recently as October 3, 1780, Greene had informed Congressman John Mathews of South Carolina that if Gates were relieved of his command due to his defeat at Camden, he would welcome the opportunity to succeed him. If Congress found it "necessary to appoint another officer to that command, and think I can be useful in that quarter, my best endeavors will not be wanting [lacking] to protect the people and serve my Country," he wrote to Mathews. He must have also discussed this prospect with Washington as well and began to hear talk among the army's officers that he might be sent southward.[10]

Though no doubt honored by Washington's trust in him, Greene also knew that his new task would be formidable. "I foresee the command will be accompanied with innumerable embarrassments," he wrote to Washington.[11] To his distant cousin Governor William Greene of Rhode Island, he also acknowledged the daunting struggles ahead. The general recalled that "a great man said; it was not in the power of mortals to command success; but he would do more; he would indeavor to deserve it."[12]

Before Greene hurriedly left West Point, he arranged for the safekeeping of his official papers, sent off his old quartermaster records to Philadelphia, and tried to borrow money for the journey from fellow officers, as he was "altogether Pennyless." Although Greene anxiously hoped that Catherine would arrive at West Point prior to his frenzied departure, she had not left Rhode Island by the time he had to ride southward "with bitter disappointment." He wrote a final letter to her before he set out. "How or when I shall return, God only knows," he said.[13]

General Greene left West Point on October 21, on an autumn journey of more than 650 miles to assume command of the Southern Department in North Carolina. He could only guess at the challenges he would face campaigning in the southern states. It would be a tenure of defeats, countless difficulties, and many frustrations but, ultimately, victory.

Chapter 1

"Our Next Operation in Consequence"

The British Move South

For I must go where lazy Peace
Will hide her drowsy head,
And, for the sport of kings, increase
The number of the dead.
—William D'Avenant, "The Soldier Going to the Field," 1644

The origins of the military campaign that ultimately led to the Battle of Guilford Courthouse on March 15, 1781, began three years earlier in 1778. It was born of disappointment and a drastically new strategic situation facing both the British government in London and the rebellious Americans.

King George III's chief ministers and military officers were frustrated that despite British Major General William Howe's early battlefield victories in 1776 around New York City, and in 1777 at Brandywine and Germantown near Philadelphia, small but persevering rebel armies were still in the field and the war dragged on. The momentous American victory near Saratoga, New York, in which an entire British army under Lieutenant General John Burgoyne surrendered to Patriot forces led by Major General Horatio Gates, had also prolonged the war. "Fifty thousand troops have not, in three years, been able to obtain secure possession of fifty miles of ground in America," a wry London newspaper quipped in 1778. Even the normally ebullient king became downcast at times at the disheartening strategic situation. "The destruction of the army of Burgoyne, and the very confined state in which [General] Howe finds himself have totally changed the face of things," Britain's monarch ruefully concluded.[14]

Great Britain's King George III.
Library of Congress.

Impatient officials of the Crown decided that after several years of not being able to crush the American rebellion in the northern and middle colonies, they would instead concentrate their efforts on defeating the disloyal insurrection in the southern American provinces. British authorities hoped that a successful invasion there would secure Georgia and the Carolinas and return them to royal authority. It was, as one modern historian concluded, "a final bid for victory in the Southern Theater."[15]

This new strategic attention on the South was embraced by Lord George Germain, who, since November 1775, was the secretary of state for the American Department. Although Frederick, Lord North, was King George's chief minister throughout the Revolutionary War, Germain was primarily responsible for directing the British war efforts in the colonies. In early December 1777, the secretary had received the shocking news of Burgoyne's surrender at Saratoga and that the Americans had not given in after their capital city, Philadelphia, had fallen to General Howe in September. Germain began conceptualizing a southern campaign in early 1778, albeit without soliciting the advice of top military commanders in America, and then started to put his plans into action.[16]

The veteran officer who would conduct the upcoming campaign in the Carolinas and Georgia was in his comfortable Philadelphia headquarters in the icy winter of 1778 when Germain's letters about the new military strategy began to arrive from London. Sir Henry Clinton officially became the British army's commander-in-chief in America in February 1778, upon the king's acceptance of the resignation of Clinton's unsuccessful predecessor, General Howe.[17] The American-born Clinton had been a soldier since 1745, and most of his service had been in the elite British Guards. He fought with distinction in the War of the Austrian Succession (1740–48) and the Seven Years' War in Europe (1756–63); during the latter conflict, he was an aide-de-camp to the Prince of Brunswick, a major British ally.[18]

Just before war broke out in America in 1775, Clinton was promoted to major general and was ordered to serve in the insurgent colonies at Boston under General Thomas Gage, then the Crown's commander-in-chief.

Left: Lord George Germain, architect of the British war efforts. *Library of Congress*.

Right: Lieutenant General Sir Henry Clinton. *Library of Congress*.

Clinton fought valiantly in the bloody battle of Bunker Hill that summer and then became Howe's second in command after Gage departed for England in October. Clinton then led a fruitless, embarrassing expedition against local Patriot forces in the Carolinas starting in January 1776 that culminated in his humiliating defeat in a joint attack on Fort Moultrie with the Royal Navy at Charleston in late June. He returned to Howe's main army in Canada and then fought conspicuously in the British victory at the Battle of Long Island, New York, in August 1776, for which he was promoted to lieutenant general and made a Knight of the Order of the Bath for leading the decisive flank attack. Clinton led a successful amphibious attack against the rebels on Manhattan Island shortly afterward and served in operations against Rhode Island, as well as in the Philadelphia Campaign in the summer and fall of 1777. No one could say he shied away from active duty.[19]

Despite his impressive heroics, Clinton was not an easy man to get along with, particularly with his superior officers in the army and his naval counterparts. He did not have an outgoing personality—he once called

The Battle of Bunker Hill, where General Clinton fought bravely near Boston in 1775. *Library of Congress.*

himself a "shy bitch"—and he was often stubborn, insistent on his own views and positions, argumentative, and paranoid. His conduct of the war became cautious and evolved into a tentative style of operations. His relations with his subordinates were often strained, particularly with Lord Cornwallis after a time. Additionally, as historian Andrew J. O'Shaughnessy has recently argued, once Clinton assumed overall command in America, he found himself in a difficult position of having to defeat Washington's army with fewer resources and troops than had his predecessor, all the while receiving little useful or timely directions from London.[20]

Soon after Germain and other British leaders began to plan for a major southern campaign, news reached them in London in March 1778 that decisively influenced how the entire war would be fought going forward: archenemy France and the fledgling United States were now allies. In Paris, representatives of King Louis XVI and the American Congress signed the Treaty of Alliance and the Treaty of Amity and Commerce on February 6, 1778, "to maintain effectually the liberty, sovereignty and independence absolute and unlimited, of the United States." This pragmatic pact was not a surprise to the British; Crown officials knew that France had been informally aiding the Americans with limited military and financial support early in the revolt. Nevertheless, the official alliance significantly shifted British priorities: going forward, Germain would have to divert limited military resources and manpower from North America to the West Indies—including soldiers, ships, and supplies—where they would be needed to defend the valuable sugar islands of the Caribbean Sea and disrupt French naval operations in American waters. Far-flung British posts in the Mediterranean, Africa, and India had to be reinforced too. The British Isles were also vulnerable to a seaborne invasion. Additionally, Crown officials knew that the French would now increase their shipments of arms, artillery, gunpowder, uniforms, and countless other desperately needed military supplies to the American army. In response, Great Britain declared war on the French on March 17, 1778.[21]

Clinton received word of the portentous treaties and the drastically changed strategic situation from London in the late spring. He knew he would have to dispatch thousands of his own troops to Canada, the West Indies, and the British post at St. Augustine in East Florida, now that the hated and opportunistic French had entered the war.[22] In order to do so, he had to consolidate his overexposed position in America. The British government decided to abandon Philadelphia, so in June 1778, Clinton elected to march his mixed force of twenty thousand British regulars, hired troops from Germany (the "Hessians"), and American Loyalists across New Jersey to their main base at New York City. Once Clinton and his army left Philadelphia, Washington ordered his army to leave its squalid camps at Valley Forge west of Philadelphia to pursue and engage the long enemy column headed northeast.[23]

The Americans caught up with Clinton's host in northern New Jersey. In a sprawling battle fought near Monmouth Courthouse on June 28, 1778, the two armies battled for hours in extreme heat until darkness, bloodshed, and exhaustion ended the contest. Clinton continued his march overnight, which allowed General Washington to claim a victory for the Americans, since the redcoats had vacated the battlefield. It was the last major battle of the war fought in the North. Once the British reached New York, General Clinton, Lord Germain, and other ministers focused instead on campaigning in the South, while Washington moved his army to camps at White Plains, New York.[24]

After the clash at Monmouth Courthouse, Clinton received word from Germain urging him to shift active operations to South Carolina and Georgia beginning in October 1778. Clinton was not happy when he read

New York City, held by the British from 1776 until the end of the war. *Library of Congress.*

the letter. He had tried unsuccessfully to resign his tiresome command several times over the past year and now had to launch this new campaign with far fewer troops than had his predecessors, in addition to maintaining a strong garrison to defend New York, a city full of Loyalist refugees. By the fall of 1778, he had 13,661 soldiers in the ranks, of whom about half were blue-coated Hessian hirelings from German principalities.[25]

In order to augment his upcoming operations in the southern theater, Clinton had to rely on the support of Americans there loyal to King George. The British plans for a decisive southern campaign rested on the widely held assumption that thousands of southern Loyalists (called "Tories" by the Patriots) would enthusiastically come forward once British troops arrived in their colonies and join forces with them to defeat the hated rebels (often known as "Whigs"). Loyalists would presumably also restore royal government and judicial systems, garrison interior posts, disarm Patriots, and capture Whig leaders. Several times prior to 1779, Loyalists in the South turned out armed and in large numbers, such as the rising of former Highland Scots along the lower Cape Fear River in North Carolina in February 1776. Although these ill-fated Tories were crushed at the Battle of Moore's Creek Bridge north of Wilmington, the king's officials still looked to this example and others as evidence that allegiance to the Crown was still widespread in the South.[26]

Military planners and ministerial officials in London placed much weight on the supposed support British forces would receive from Loyalists in the South. Exiled Americans in London often provided exaggerated reports to the king's ministers regarding the number of southerners in the Carolinas and Georgia who were waiting to rise up and join British efforts to subdue the rebellion. Recent research has suggested that "the British officials were indeed correct in believing that large numbers of Loyalists inhabited Georgia and South Carolina, and that they would contribute greatly to the effort to restore royal authority in those provinces." However, reliance on these loyal subjects to contribute to British victory proved to be unrealistic for many British officers during the war, including in the South. Under the assumption that much support awaited the Crown's troops, plans for southern military operations proceeded.[27]

As ordered, General Clinton renewed British campaigning in the South in the late fall of 1778, conscious that every soldier he deployed weakened the garrison at New York, which Washington's Continentals threatened from their positions north of the fortified city. Clinton began with a modest effort to capture a rebel-held port. In November 1778, the British commander sent three thousand troops led by Lieutenant Colonel Archibald Campbell to take Savannah, Georgia.[28] The British soundly defeated Major General Robert Howe's frightened American force outside Savannah on December 29 and captured the town after the rebels ignominiously fled the battlefield. Several weeks later, Campbell was joined by one thousand redcoats from St. Augustine, Florida, under Major General Augustine Prévost, who had marched north to Savannah and thereby secured the Georgia coast on his way.[29]

With Savannah captured and thousands of the king's troops now in Georgia, it was time to find out if southern Loyalists would come forward in the wake of Campbell's victory. The optimistic British were not disappointed. Colonel Campbell recruited, armed, and organized hundreds of eager Loyalists into militia companies around Savannah. The British brought order to coastal Georgia, as many cowed Patriots kept a low profile or fled west to the backcountry, particularly to Augusta on the upper Savannah River. Campbell marched part of his troops there in late January 1779 and occupied that important backcountry settlement. While at Augusta, he was joined by about 1,400 armed Loyalists, a considerable force in that frontier section of the province.

It began to look like Germain's assumptions about Loyalist support were true. However, a growing Whig threat in the backcountry by mid-February led Campbell to evacuate Augusta and move to the coast. This served to highlight perhaps the greatest problem British officers continually faced while campaigning in the South: without strong, sustained military support in the form of redcoats and forts in their neighborhoods, Loyalists would invariably face the danger of Whig retaliatory attacks once the British soldiers left.[30] As one modern military historian has observed, the British army had "an unhappy tradition of abandoning its valuable loyalist allies, thus further undermining whatever indigenous support existed for the reestablishment of royal authority."[31]

The early months of 1779 proved to be a mixed bag for the Patriots trying to counter the British invasion of the South. American forces met with a battlefield success in backcountry Georgia on February 14, at Kettle Creek, northwest of Augusta. A few weeks later, however, a large Whig force of 1,100 militia suffered a stinging defeat at Brier Creek near Augusta at the hands of an aggressive British force led by Lieutenant Colonel James M. Prévost, who had replaced Colonel Campbell and was the younger brother of the general.[32]

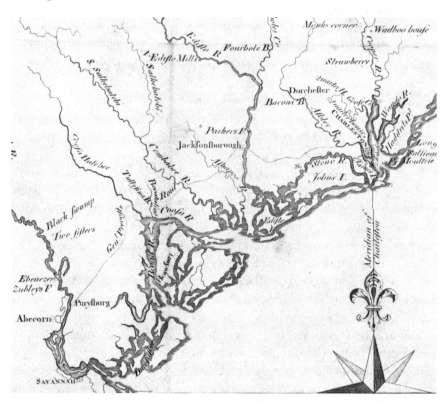

The coastal South from Savannah (*lower left*) to Charleston (*upper right*). *Library of Congress.*

Meanwhile, Major General Benjamin Lincoln of Massachusetts, the new Continental commander of the Southern Department as of September 1778, worked feverishly to rebuild a small Patriot army around Black Swamp, South Carolina, along the Savannah River, assisted by his second in command, Brigadier General William Moultrie, a prominent South Carolina officer and politician. On April 30, at Black Swamp, General Prévost attacked Moultrie's small militia force, which was at the time detached from Lincoln's main body, operating closer to Augusta. When Moultrie's troops, reinforced by several thousand rebel militiamen under South Carolina governor John Rutledge, had retreated east to Charleston by May 8, the British pursued them with 2,500 men and threatened the city. Lincoln's approaching troops, however, led a wary Prévost to prudently withdraw from the Charleston area southward to Savannah in mid-May, lest he be caught too far from his base.

The first several months of 1779 showed Prévost and Clinton that British troops in sufficient numbers could campaign in the southern theater and encourage Loyalists to join them. However, the operations gained no territory for the Crown, provoked numerous musket-wielding Whigs to embody for their own defense, and left the Tories dangerously vulnerable. As historian John S. Pancake concluded, "[A] show of force by the British was useless unless it could be demonstrated that the authority of the Crown was permanent."[33]

After a bloody but largely indecisive battle on June 20 at Stono Ferry, thirteen miles west of Charleston, a lull in operations developed during the months of summer heat. Then on September 1, a large French fleet with four thousand French soldiers aboard arrived from the West Indies off British-held Savannah, to the astonishment and relief of their new American allies. The French were commanded by the Comte d'Estaing, who conferred with General Lincoln in Charleston. The two commanders agreed on a joint attack against Savannah. Lincoln marched one thousand Continentals and twice as many militia soldiers south into Georgia to meet the well-drilled French force. The Franco-American army invested the city

The Hon.ble B. LINCOLN, Esq

Major General in the American Army

Major General Benjamin Lincoln surrendered Charleston and his army to the British in May 1780. *Library of Congress.*

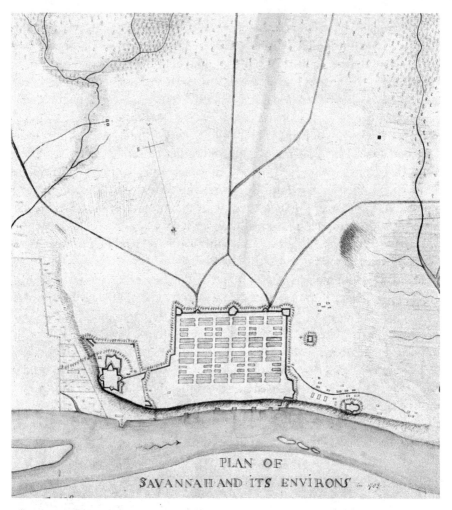

PLAN OF
SAVANNAH AND ITS ENVIRONS in 402

The extensive British defenses of Savannah, Georgia, shown here in 1782. *Library of Congress.*

in September but could not force the stubborn enemy to capitulate. Growing impatient, on October 9, the allies imprudently stormed the strong British fortifications defended by just under five thousand men. Heavy casualties among the brave attackers in a ruinous charge against British earthworks at Spring Hill led the two commanders to suspend any further assaults. General Lincoln and most of his despondent men returned to Charleston nine days later; soon thereafter, the French sailed away.

The defense of Savannah was a significant victory for the British, and Prévost's success further encouraged General Clinton in New York and

Lord Germain in London to launch a more powerful campaign in the South during the cooler months. "I think this is the greatest event that has happened the whole war," Sir Henry crowed, and "I need not say what will be our next operation in consequence."[34]

The "next operation" Clinton cryptically wrote about was by eighteenth-century standards a staggering logistical undertaking. Over the next several months, the British in New York organized thousands of soldiers and sailors, collected scores of boats, gathered massive amounts of food and fodder, and bet on good weather for a major seaborne thrust to capture Charleston and restore royal government to South Carolina. Once achieved, Clinton would sail back to New York with most of his troops, leaving behind a smaller force as a nucleus around which Loyalists would rally. Accompanying the expedition was Clinton's second in command, Lord Cornwallis, along with a bold young dragoon officer named Banastre Tarleton, of whom much would be heard in the coming months.

After embarking from New York Harbor with almost nine thousand troops cramped on ninety transport ships guarded by a small fleet of the Royal Navy, Clinton's closely packed armada set sail on December 26, 1779. Lashing winter storms and rough seas scattered the fleet in the Atlantic, but after several weeks, British ships began to appear off the Georgia coast near Savannah.

Once most of the battered expedition reunited, Clinton landed his sea-soaked forces twenty miles south of Charleston, beginning on February 11, 1780. Slowly moving his army northward on sandy roads in the face of scattered but ineffectual resistance by American forces, Clinton's army began laying a formal siege to Charleston on April 1. General Lincoln chose to defend the city from behind extensive earthworks manned by a garrison of about 5,600 Continentals and southern militia soldiers. He gambled and lost. Eventually, Lincoln surrendered the pummeled garrison on May 12, a blow so strongly felt that Congress in Philadelphia ordered an inquiry into Lincoln's conduct of the campaign.[35]

Charleston's fall was arguably the Patriots' worst military disaster of the war. Thousands of irreplaceable Continental troops were captured, as well as artillery pieces, supplies, and munitions. Patriot morale suffered a setback in the siege's aftermath, just as southern Loyalists could now breathe easier. Moreover, Charleston could be used as a strong base to support future British land and sea campaigns against the French sugar islands in the Caribbean. Most alarming for the Patriot cause, however, was that the vanquished southern American provinces were now open to

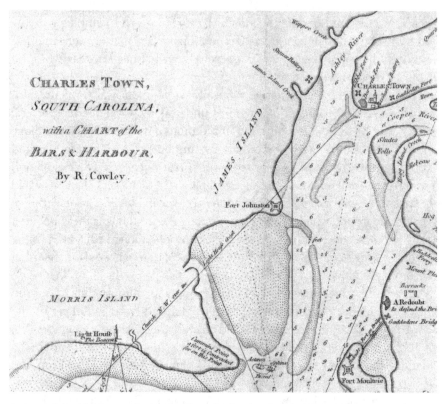

A chart of the Charleston, South Carolina vicinity showing the city's defenses as well. *Library of Congress.*

British conquest and occupation, given the lack of an army in the field to oppose them.

Not all of those fighting for American independence gave up hope for the cause, however, one of whom was the Continental Army's indefatigable commander-in-chief. General Washington acknowledged that Charleston's fall "will no doubt give spirit to our Enemies." Yet he also believed that the setback would only have "a temporary effect upon our Affairs" and that "if extensively considered and rightly improved, it may be attended in the end by happy consequences." Washington presciently observed that the British in America were overextending themselves by engaging in a southern campaign, especially now that the French had entered the war. "The enemy," he wrote to the governor of Connecticut, "by attempting to hold conquests so remote [from one another], must dissipate their force, and of course afford [the American army] opportunities of striking one or the other extremity."[36] He also hoped that the defeat would have an inspirational effect on American Patriots. "If we exert ourselves virtuously and as we are able," he wrote to a Massachusetts correspondent, it could "rouse us from the…unaccountable state of security in which we were sunk. Heaven grant the blow may have this effect. If it should, the misfortune may prove a benefit and the means of saving us."[37]

Time and effort were needed to determine if Washington would be proven right.

Chapter 2

"THIS MISERABLE COUNTRY"

Cornwallis in the Carolinas

Thou art my battle axe and weapon of war: for with thee will I break in pieces
the nations, with thee I will destroy kingdoms.
—Jeremiah, 51:20 (King James Version)

The salient British victory at Charleston crushed Patriot resistance in the South for months. Thousands of Virginia, Carolina, and Georgia militia surrendered there, as did almost all Continental battalions in the Southern Department. Active support for the Revolutionary struggle against Great Britain naturally waned in much of the theater. Proof of this sagging morale was easy to see in and around Charleston soon after the captive American garrison became prisoners. Thousands of relieved Loyalists came into the port city to swear oaths of allegiance in front of British officials, including a number of prominent wealthy planters who had previously supported independence. Many of these vengeful Tories now volunteered to support the repression of the American rebels in their midst who had done the same to them just months before.

General Clinton was initially lenient toward the southern Whigs for the most part. Recognizing that captured militiamen would only consume his supplies and posed little threat if turned loose, Clinton paroled them to their homes and farms on their sworn oaths that they would not serve the Patriot cause militarily until officially exchanged with British prisoners of war. Many Continental officers were paroled too, including General Lincoln. The Continental regulars, however, were held in captivity, to be formally exchanged later.[38]

SOUTH-CAROLINA.

By Sir *HENRY CLINTON*, Knight of the Bath, General of His Majesty's Forces, and *MARIOT ARBUTHNOT*, Esquire, Vice-Admiral of the Blue, His Majesty's Commissioners to restore Peace and good Government in the several Colonies in Rebellion in North-America.

PROCLAMATION.

HIS MAJESTY having been pleased, by His Letters Patent, under the Great Seal of Great-Britain, to appoint us to be his Commissioners, to restore the Blessings of Peace and Liberty to the several Colonies in Rebellion in America, WE do hereby make public his most gracious Intentions, and in Obedience to his Commands, DO DECLARE, to such of his deluded Subjects, as have been perverted from their Duty by the Factious Arts of self-interested and ambitious Men, That they will still be received with Mercy and Forgiveness, if they immediately return to their Allegiance, and a due Obedience to those Laws and that Government which they formerly boasted was their best Birthright and noblest Inheritance, and upon a due Experience of the Sincerity of their Professions, a full and free Pardon will be granted for the treasonable Offences which they have heretofore committed, in such Manner and Form as his Majesty's Commission doth direct.

NEVERTHELESS, it is only to those, who, convinced of their Errors, are firmly resolved to return to and Support that Government under which they were formerly so happy and free, that these gracious Offers are once more renewed, and therefore those Persons are excepted, who, notwithstanding their present hopeless Situation, and regardless of the accumulating Pressure of the Miseries of the People, which their infatuated Conduct must contribute to increase, are nevertheless still so hardened in their Guilt, as to endeavour to keep alive the Flame of Rebellion in this Province, which will otherwise soon be reinstated in its former Prosperity, Security, and Peace:

Nor can we at present resolve to extend the Royal Clemency to those who are poluted with the Blood of their Fellow Citizens, most wantonly and inhumanly shed under the mock Forms of Justice, because they refused Submission to an Usurpation which they abhorred, and would not oppose that Government with which they deemed themselves inseparably connected: And in order to give Quiet and Content to the Minds of his Majesty's faithful and well affected Subjects, WE do again assure them, that they shall have effectual Countenance, Protection and Support, and as soon as the Situation of the Province will admit, the Inhabitants will be reinstated in the Possession of all those Rights and Immunities which they heretofore enjoyed under a free British Government, exempt from Taxation, except by their own Legislature: And we do hereby call upon all his Majesty's faithful Subjects to be aiding with their Endeavours, in order that a Measure, so conducive to their own Happiness, and the Welfare and Prosperity of the Province, may be the more speedily and easily attained.

GIVEN under our Hands and Seals, at Charles-Town, the First Day of June, in the Twentieth Year of His Majesty's Reign and in the Year of Our Lord One Thousand Seven Hundred and Eighty.

HENRY CLINTON,

MARIOT ARBUTHNOT.

By their EXCELLENCY's Command,

JAMES SIMPSON, *Secretary.*

CHARLES-TOWN: Printed by ROBERTSON, MACDONALD & CAMERON, in Broad-Street, the Corner of Church-Street.

Clinton's first proclamation after the 1780 fall of Charleston, in which he called on rebels to swear allegiance to King George III. *Library of Congress.*

Clinton and his officers were looking for the Loyalists to do more than just swear an oath of loyalty to the king in the weeks after Charleston surrendered. Since Clinton planned to return to New York with much of his army, he expected armed Loyalists to assemble into militia companies in order to augment British and Hessian regulars. To lead the organization of Loyalist volunteers, he appointed a young Scottish regular officer, Major Patrick Ferguson, to the position of inspector of militia in the southern theater. Once armed and accoutered, Ferguson's Loyalist units were to act as a police force, administer loyalty oaths to former rebels, and restore the king's authority across the provinces, particularly in the vast Carolina backcountry. The initial efforts led by Major Ferguson were remarkably successful. By the end of June, the British had organized thousands of Loyalists into military companies, mostly in South Carolina.[39]

Clinton, however, compounded the challenges the British would face in conquering the South with a political blunder. Shortly before he departed for New York, he issued a new proclamation that, in effect, rescinded his earlier announced leniency and now required all Whigs to fully support the king, including taking up arms for the British. Those who would not serve militarily in the field would be treated as outlaws and rebels. Some Americans who had earlier pledged allegiance to royal authority regarded this announcement as breaking the terms of the paroles they previously swore after the fall of Charleston; many felt no longer restricted by their oaths and rejoined the Whig forces.[40]

Clinton sailed for New York on June 8. With little remaining enthusiasm for the war in America, he had expected to return to England after his southern campaign against Charleston, but when his request to resign was finally allowed by Germain, he instead declined it in the wake of his successful Carolina operations. This *volte face* surprised and angered Cornwallis, who expected to become commander-in-chief in America once Clinton left America for England. In fact, a long-simmering feud between the two generals had boiled over during the siege, during which their relationship became so estranged that Cornwallis asked Clinton not to consult him further on operational matters. No doubt Cornwallis was glad to see his superior officer sail off, leaving him an independent command with about four thousand troops.[41]

The British general destined to face Nathanael Greene in battle at Guilford Courthouse less than a year later was a veteran soldier in the American war by the time he assumed command of the king's southern troops in June 1780. Lord Cornwallis came from a landed Suffolk family, born on the last

Lieutenant General Charles, Lord Cornwallis, the British commander at the Battles of Camden and Guilford Courthouse. *Library of Congress.*

day of 1738. He attended Eton College as a youth and served in the army's prestigious 1st Regiment of Foot Guards in Germany during the Seven Years' War. That made him "an experienced veteran of European warfare before his arrival in America" when the Revolutionary War commenced, wrote O'Shaughnessy, a modern historian of the British commanders in the conflict. Cornwallis was also a politician and entered the House of Commons in 1760. Two years later, upon his father's death, he assumed the title of 2nd Earl Cornwallis and became a member of the House of Lords, although he still held his army commission and became the colonel of the 33rd Regiment of Foot, a distinguished battalion.[42]

In 1775, as war in America loomed, Cornwallis was promoted to the rank of major general. Although he did not favor a military solution to the imperial crisis, he volunteered to serve in the rebellious colonies once war erupted. After embarking at Cork, Ireland, he arrived with British reinforcements for Clinton at Cape Fear, North Carolina, in 1776 and then served with Sir Henry in the latter's unsuccessful attempt to capture Charleston in June of that year, during which the two generals were on good terms. Cornwallis fought in the battles against Washington's troops around New York City beginning in August 1776, in which the American commander and his rapidly diminishing army were forced to abandon the city in November, hurriedly retreat across northern New Jersey, and cross the Delaware River into Pennsylvania. The Continental Army struck back on December 26, however, when Washington won a small but morale-boosting victory against an unsuspecting Hessian garrison at Trenton, New Jersey. General Howe ordered Cornwallis to march several thousand redcoats to ensnare the Americans, but Washington managed not only to elude Cornwallis but also win another improbable victory against a British detachment at Princeton, New Jersey, on January 3, 1777. For Cornwallis, it was not a successful few weeks of traipsing about the frozen roads and fields of New Jersey.[43]

The 1777 battle of Brandywine, Pennsylvania, where Cornwallis distinguished himself leading a flank attack on Washington's army. *Library of Congress.*

One of Cornwallis's finest days as a field commander came in Pennsylvania in the late summer of 1777, when he led the British army's devastating flanking maneuver at the Battle of Brandywine on September 11. There General Howe defeated Washington's Continentals and soon afterward captured the American capital, Philadelphia. That fall, Cornwallis returned to Great Britain, where he arrived in January 1778 and had an audience with King George, during which the general frankly expressed his opinion that the war in America could not be won and the colonies could not be conquered. Although the king did not agree with the earl's bleak assessment, he appreciated Cornwallis's honesty and past service, which he honored by promoting Cornwallis to lieutenant general and by giving him a dormant commission to succeed Clinton as commander-in-chief in North America in the event of the latter's death, disability, or recall. Clinton obviously concurred with the Crown's favorable assessment of Cornwallis's abilities, as he later wrote that "if the endeavors of any man are likely, under the present prospects, to be attended with success, Lord Cornwallis, for many reasons, stands among the first."[44]

Cornwallis returned to America in the spring of 1778 and fought at the Battle of Monmouth Courthouse in late June. Afterward, while in New York with the main British host, he received a letter that chilled his heart—his

General George Washington. *Library of Congress.*

beloved wife, Jemima, was gravely ill at the family home in Suffolk. He sailed immediately for England, but Jemima died about one month after Cornwallis reached their home. Despondent after his wife's death, the general decided to return to America to spare himself the painful reminders of his love had he remained at home.[45]

The grieving general was back in America in July 1779 and was initially welcomed by Clinton. Tension soon rose between the two, however, as Cornwallis expected Clinton to depart for London at any time, once the latter resigned his command. Cornwallis also recalled that Clinton put much of the blame for the defeats at Trenton and Princeton on Cornwallis's shoulders, which added to the increasingly strained relations between the army's top two generals within the defenses of New York City.[46]

Despite this uneasy command situation, Clinton launched his massive expedition against Charleston in December 1779. Cornwallis went along as second in command, and as noted earlier, the city's garrison surrendered on May 12, 1780. By that time, the two British generals were barely on speaking terms; Cornwallis, in fact, had asked Germain to give him a new assignment anywhere but under Clinton's authority the day after Lincoln capitulated. By June, however, this had become unnecessary when Clinton returned to New York with most of his soldiers, a major military victory to his credit, and his troubles with Cornwallis hundreds of ocean miles behind him. "I leave Lord Cornwallis here with a sufficient force to keep it [Charleston] against the world," Sir Henry wrote upon his departure, unless "a superior [French] fleet shows itself, in which case I shall despair of ever seeing peace restored to this miserable country."[47]

Once in command at Charleston, Cornwallis faced a daunting task. He had to restore royal authority to South Carolina so that a functioning civil government would once again be in place. Rebellious Whigs had to be disarmed, kept at home, and made to swear allegiance to King George. He also had to maintain the territorial and political gains made in Georgia and keep that rebellious province secure in the face of hostile Whig militia

A view of Charleston, the South's largest city, in the eighteenth century. *Library of Congress.*

forces. Employing Major Ferguson, the general also needed to arm and equip Loyalist militia units in South Carolina to keep it under British control. "Success at Charleston, unless followed in the back country, will be of little avail," Clinton had instructed him the week after the American surrender. His Lordship had to do all these things with a reduced force too, since Clinton took many veteran redcoats and Hessians back to New York in June. And Cornwallis had to accomplish these tasks before he could attempt any operations into North Carolina, according to Clinton's instructions.[48]

The British were nothing if not tenacious. Within days of Lincoln's surrender, Crown forces had quickly marched to occupy key towns of the South Carolina interior, frontier, and coast. Redcoats established fortified posts at Georgetown on the Atlantic north of Charleston, along with Ninety Six, Rocky Mount, and Camden in the remote backcountry. They set up garrisons at Orangeburg, seventy-five miles northwest of Charleston on the Edisto River, and at Cheraw on the Pee Dee River, less than ten miles from the North Carolina border. British troops also garrisoned Augusta. With Continental forces defeated and Whig militiamen dispersed, the king's soldiers now seemed to have conquered South Carolina.[49]

It was during the early months of the South Carolina Campaign that one of Cornwallis's young subalterns began to make a name for himself. Lieutenant Colonel Banastre Tarleton, a twenty-six-year-old cavalryman from a successful Liverpool mercantile family, had squandered thousands of pounds of an inheritance gambling and living *la dolce vita* in London instead of studying law before obtaining a commission in the 1st King's Dragoon Guards. In early 1776, he voluntarily joined Cornwallis's venture with Clinton to Cape Fear and then returned to New York later that summer. Tarleton came to serve under Colonel William, Lord Cathcart, in a Loyalist battalion called the British Legion, a mixed force of green-coated, leather-helmeted cavalry and infantry recruited among Americans who remained adherents to George III. In December 1779, when the British Legion joined Clinton's massive expedition to South Carolina, Tarleton was the battalion's field commander.[50]

Before Lincoln surrendered Charleston, the aggressive Tarleton won a notable victory at the head of his Legion at Monck's Corner on April 14, 1780. There, his command struck several hundred Continentals under Brigadier General Isaac Huger, who were surprised in their camps. The victory also helped cut off Lincoln's garrison from other American units operating outside of Charleston's battered siege lines.[51]

Tarleton added to his growing reputation as a hard-hitting cavalry commander capable of operating independently with a subsequent victory a few weeks later on the Santee River. On May 6, 1780, at Lenud's Ferry,

Hard-hitting cavalryman Banastre Tarleton was one of Cornwallis's most effective officers but suffered a defeat at Cowpens in 1781. *Library of Congress.*

forty-five miles north of Charleston, Lieutenant Colonel Anthony Walton White and his 1st Continental Light Dragoons were encamped with Lieutenant Colonel William Washington's 3rd Continental Light Dragoons and a small contingent of North Carolinians. Tarleton's dragoons suddenly attacked them in the afternoon before expected Virginia reinforcements under Colonel Abraham Buford could support them. Once again, a bold strike on an unsuspecting American force led to a British victory and came to characterize Tarleton's martial *modus operandi*.[52]

The most controversial engagement in which Tarleton commanded British forces during the war was at the rural settlement of

Whig sympathizers in the Waxhaws District in upcountry South Carolina on May 29, 1780. There, Tarleton's dragoons attacked a contingent of Virginia Continentals after their American commander, Colonel Buford, rejected his call for surrender. The British cavalry charged the Continentals, who waited too long to fire their first volley. Tarleton's horse was killed from under him, and some British dragoons thought their commander had been shot after the Americans had surrendered, which infuriated them and led to a brutal, slashing attack. The Patriots suffered heavy casualties, and many were killed unarmed before the Legion's officers could quiet the dragoons. Some rebels did, in fact, shoot at the enemy after the surrender was started, but they may not have known that the fighting was over in the confusion of battle.

After the engagement, Tarleton was cited by many American military officers for the brutality of his troops and their alleged inhumane slaughter of Continental soldiers after they had surrendered. "Bloody Ban" became his nom de guerre, and "Tarleton's Quarter" was now synonymous with taking no prisoners. Modern historians, writers, and even filmmakers continue to echo and exaggerate these claims of cruelty on the part of Tarleton and the British Legion, even though, in the words of historian Jim Piecuch, "firsthand accounts of the event are scarce, and their validity must be carefully evaluated." Nevertheless, young Tarleton's fearsome reputation for showing his enemies no mercy became widespread at the war progressed.[53]

The fall of Charleston and ensuing British efforts to establish far-flung military posts throughout South Carolina did not crush all Patriot forces in the South, nor did they prevent Carolina Whigs from mustering and taking the field to fight the hated Tories and redcoats. After Buford's crushing defeat at the Waxhaws, Patriots won small but encouraging victories at Alexander's Old Field and Mobley's Meeting House, both in South Carolina, and at Ramsour's Mill, North Carolina, where that summer armed Loyalists were routed and suffered heavy casualties. In July, an unguarded detachment of Tarleton's Legion suffered a blow at the hands of Whig militia at Williamson's Plantation (called "Huck's Defeat"), near today's Rock Hill, South Carolina, on the twelfth.

Balancing these small victories, Whigs endured setbacks against the Tories as well in a bitter ongoing struggle that was turning in to an internecine war. Greene noted early in his tenure that the "whole country is in danger of being laid waste by the Whigs and Torrys, who pursue each other with as much relentless fury as beasts of prey." As modern historian John S. Pancake wrote in his study of the final campaign in the South, "what erupted in the summer of 1780 from the Savannah to the North Carolina border was a bloody civil war. Old feuds were settled under the banner of patriotism, and British hopes for a peaceful occupation vanished in the smoke of burning barns and houses." North Carolina also experienced the same cruel Whig-Tory clashes in the coming two years as well; in June 1781, Governor Thomas Burke would observe that the war had "unhappily kindled the most fierce and vindictive animosity" between Whigs and Tories, characterized by "reciprocal violences and bloodshed."[54] This vicious civil war became the omnipresent background against which the regular armies' military operations were fought until 1783.

Chapter 3

"A Severe Rebuke"

Gates and the Disaster at Camden

Then "spur and sword" was the battle word, and we made the helmets ring
Shouting like madmen all the while "for God and for the King!"
And though they snuffed psalms, to give the rebel dogs their due
When the roaring shot poured thick and hot, they were stalwart men and true
—cavalier ballad, English Civil War, 1643

The Continental Congress appointed Major General Horatio Gates on June 13, 1780, to lead the Southern Department soon after learning that Lincoln surrendered Charleston. Reliable news of the capitulation and the strength of Patriot forces in the department was scarce in Philadelphia. Given the lack of firm knowledge of the disordered military situation in the South, Samuel Huntington—then serving as the president of Congress—advised Gates to rely on "your own prudence and experience" in assuming this new responsibility. This ambiguous guidance could not have been very encouraging to the newly appointed southern commander.[55]

When choosing a replacement for Lincoln, congressional leaders easily landed on the most successful Continental Army general of the war to date. Gates had commanded the American forces at Saratoga, where Burgoyne surrendered to him on October 17, 1777, in what one historian described as "one of the crucial battles of American and world history" and "the turning point of the Revolution." Gates's victory not only eliminated an entire enemy army of almost six thousand soldiers but also convinced

France to enter the war on the side of the Americans in early 1778. Although some scholars have dubiously argued that Gates's role was more as a coordinator than a combat leader, without question he successfully commanded the Patriot army (including a large contingent of northern militia) during the decisive autumn campaign, which was largely a cautious, defensive operation that compelled Burgoyne to surrender after two pitched battles along the Hudson River. Popular with his troops and now the winner of the greatest Patriot victory in the war to date, Gates was a hero throughout the American states. Therefore, when Congress looked for a new general for the South in 1780, it naturally turned to Gates, who was at that time residing unassigned at his farm since late 1779.[56]

Major General Horatio Gates, who was replaced by Greene in December 1780. *Library of Congress.*

Gates had other salient qualities to recommend him. Born in 1727 in England, he was a former British army officer who served in America during the French and Indian War (1754–63). During that struggle between Britain and France and both of their Indian allies, Gates fought alongside General Edward Braddock in a grueling 1755 wilderness campaign to capture Fort Duquesne, held by the French in the Ohio country. The arduous expedition, in which Washington also served as a volunteer aide, ended in utter disaster several miles from modern Pittsburgh, and Gates was wounded in the debacle against Indian warriors and French officers. He returned briefly to England after the war, but in 1772, he came back to America and took up residence near the upper Potomac River in Berkeley County, Virginia. When the Revolutionary War broke out, Gates sided with the Patriot cause and began his Continental military service in 1775.

In 1776, Gates won acclaim for turning back an enemy thrust up Lake Champlain in northern New York, but his spectacular triumph the following year at Saratoga made him a shining star. His success, however, embroiled him in a murky political struggle within the Continental Army's leadership and also involved Congress. Whether intentional or not, Gates failed to report the victory at Saratoga directly to his commander, General Washington. Rather, he sent the news to Congress, from which Washington

General Gates won a salient victory in 1777 at Saratoga, where British General Burgoyne surrendered his army to him. *Library of Congress*.

officially learned of Gates's wilderness success. This was a major breach of military protocol by Gates, who knew better. It also annoyed Washington, always sensitive to criticism, particularly since he had lost the Battles of Brandywine and Germantown, in Pennsylvania, at the same time Gates was waging his victorious campaign in the deep forests of New York. Gates was also slow to return troops Washington had sent him and wanted back with his own army.[57]

Also that fall, a group of senior Continental officers and their aides began to circulate the idea that the victorious Gates should replace the ineffective Washington as commander-in-chief, as the Virginian's last victory (at Princeton) had been almost a year earlier. This opposition—which included some calculating congressmen—centered on Brigadier General Thomas Conway, a scheming Frenchman in Continental service, so that the hushed talk and rumors of conspiracy has come down in history as "the Conway Cabal." Conway had written a private letter to Gates calling Washington "a weak general" that was inadvertently leaked to one of Washington's supporters by Gates's aide-de-camp. An insulted Washington learned of this unflattering sentiment against him, which may actually have been much less organized than assumed at the time (and since), and suspected that Gates supported it. In the end, Washington was not replaced, but he maintained a wary suspicion of Gates's questionable motives from then on.[58]

Congress's appointment of Gates to the southern theater command was made without Washington's approval. Nevertheless, the "Hero of Saratoga" set out to take charge of the department in the aftermath of the fall of Charleston, hoping to regroup, feed, and resupply whatever tattered forces were left in the South.

If Gates did not already know of the enormous difficulties he would face in the Carolinas and Virginia upon his appointment, he soon began to receive unsettling warnings. "Whilst I congratulate you on your present unanimous appointment to the command of the Southern Department," wrote Pennsylvania congressman John Armstrong to the general, "I cannot be insensible to the prospects before you and the many known and unknown difficulties you have to encounter."[59] American Major General Charles Lee is said to have told Gates, "[T]ake care that you do not exchange Northern laurels for Southern willows." It did not take long for the veteran Gates to learn how poor fortunes were in the South for the cause of independence in the long war's sixth summer. By the time he reached Fredericksburg, Virginia, he learned that he would command "an army without strength—a military chest without money. A department apparently deficient in public spirit, and a climate that increases despondency instead of animating the soldier's arm." Riding farther south to Richmond, he found there nothing to encourage him. Virginia's governor, Thomas Jefferson, could offer little more than encouragement and promises to the new southern commander.[60]

Once in North Carolina, Gates found even more difficulties. In a long letter to Governor Jefferson, the general decried the deplorable situation he found upon reaching Hillsborough in mid-July. Gates must have been dumbfounded by what he found:

> When I had the honor of seeing your Excellency at Richmond I was taught to look forward to much difficulty and a perplexed department, yet I cannot but profess that, in the course of a long and often critical service, it has hitherto never fallen to my lot to witness a scene of such multiplied and increasing wants, as my present command exhibits. Of the Militia voted by your State only 1438 are now upon the ground[,] Commissioned and Non Commissioned Officers included and Those not so compleatly supplied as I either wish'd or expected. The arms were yesterday distributed among them, a few out of repair, but too many without cartouch-boxes, and all destitute of bayonet belts[,] which I need scarcely tell your Excellency is the certain loss of the bayonet. They are deficient also in hatchets or light axes....

Thomas Jefferson, Virginia's beleaguered governor from 1779 to 1781. *Library of Congress.*

These defects are however but trifling when compared to the weightier considerations of Arms, ammunition and provision....Upon the subject of provisions my reports must be still less satisfactory...there are often intervals of 24 hours in which the army without distinction are obliged to feed upon such green vegetables as they can find, having neither animal food or corn. So frequent and total a want, must eventually break up our camp, should not the evil be hastily remedied, and has unfortunately arose from several causes, one of which can alone be corrected. The scarcity of Crops for the last year, the disaffection of many of the inhabitants and a want of economy, and management. The supplies have been precariously obtain'd by detachments from the Army whose misapplied violence in some instances must affect any future purchase.[61]

Nevertheless, Gates and his small staff pressed on southward until the warm night of July 24, when they reached the American army's camp at Coxe's Mill along the Deep River (near modern Ramseur).[62] Gates found there a mixed force of ragged militia, regulars, and cavalry, including 1,400 Maryland and Delaware Continentals who had been sent south from New Jersey in 1780 to help defend Charleston but only made it to Virginia before that city surrendered. This small, poorly equipped force was led by Major General "Baron" Johann de Kalb, a fifty-nine-year-old Frenchman with vast military experience in Europe and trusted by Washington but not, in fact, a titled noble. A force of more than 1,000 badly armed North Carolina militia led by Major General Richard Caswell, a former (and first) governor of the state, was operating to the south on the Yadkin River. He eventually joined Gates, as did 700 ill-equipped Virginians under Brigadier General Edward Stevens, a few weeks later.[63]

Against the prudent advice of his new subordinate officers and under pressure from southern political leaders to begin active operations immediately, Gates almost instantly decided to march from Coxe's Mill on the Deep River directly toward Camden in South Carolina, an enemy stronghold commanded by Colonel Francis, Lord Rawdon, a capable young officer of extensive experience in the war. This direct route would take the army "thro' a thin settled," desolate, Tory-infested country, with limited supplies for the troops.[64] Gates's incredulous officers instead urged him to move against Camden by way of Charlotte to the west, where food and fodder would be more plentiful amid more numerous Whig sympathizers. But Gates insisted on marching by the more direct route, and by August 14, he had more than four thousand hungry, sick, and footsore men situated at Rugeley's Mill, about twelve miles north of Camden, to threaten the British.[65] The worn-out men had "very little other subsistence than a short allowance of fresh beef, green corn, apples, and peaches."[66]

Once Gates had been reinforced by Steven's militia by the fourteenth, he decided to move his army south several miles to take up a better

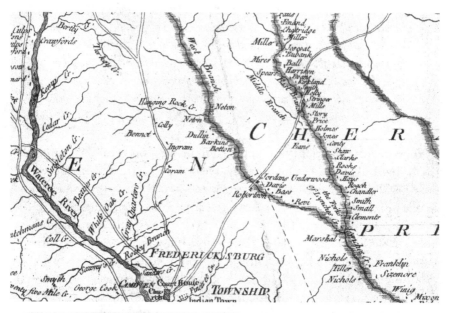

Above: Gates marched his army directly toward Camden (bottom) from the north, against his veteran officers' advice. *Library of Congress.*

Left: Major General Horatio Gates. *Library of Congress.*

defensive position behind Gum Swamp on the sandy road to Camden. At ten o'clock on the night of August 15, he ordered his men to make a night march to occupy this new line, which he figured would entice the redcoats to attack him.[67]

While Gates and his troops approached Camden in the darkness, Lord Cornwallis had already arrived at the small, fortified village on the fourteenth and took stock of the sickly garrison. He had at hand three tough regiments of veteran British regulars, four companies of light infantry, Tarleton's Legion, two Loyalist regiments, and several Tory militia companies from the Carolinas. Most of these units, however, were understrength, as active campaigning in the humid South and sickness in the water-logged camps had taken their toll. All told, Cornwallis had just under two thousand effectives at the fortified town.[68]

The British general decided that he would attack Gates as the exhausted Patriot force approached Camden. By coincidence, Cornwallis ordered his men forward at ten o'clock on the night of the fifteenth, as did Gates, so that the lead elements of the two opposing armies slammed into each other on the road in total darkness at about 2:30 a.m. on the sixteenth. After recoiling in confusion, the armies set about establishing their lines for the battle both knew would come at dawn. Cornwallis placed his regular regiments on his right flank, east of the road that bisected the sandy battleground, shaded by tall pines. He posted the Loyalist battalions on his left, two battalions of the 71st Foot in a second line in support, and Tarleton's Legion in reserve.[69]

Gates, however, made a fatal mistake in deploying his men, an error that he never explained and has puzzled historians ever since. The Continental general placed his most experienced troops—the 2nd Maryland and the small Delaware Regiment—on his right, with the 1st Maryland Regiment in reserve behind them. However, he placed the North Carolina militia in the center and Virginia militia to the left, both of which were far less reliable than the veteran Continentals. This questionable deployment was probably influenced by the fact that the weary troops had been in column as they marched south in the dark just hours beforehand, and American officers had little time or opportunity to situate the army more effectively, particularly since the lines of the two armies were so close. The successful use of militia troops in battle would be a key factor in the Battles of Cowpens and Guilford Courthouse in the winter of 1781 and was influenced by the results of the fighting near Camden.[70]

Unfortunately for Gates, situating the unpredictable militia companies in his center and on the left flank led to disaster. The British right-flank troops

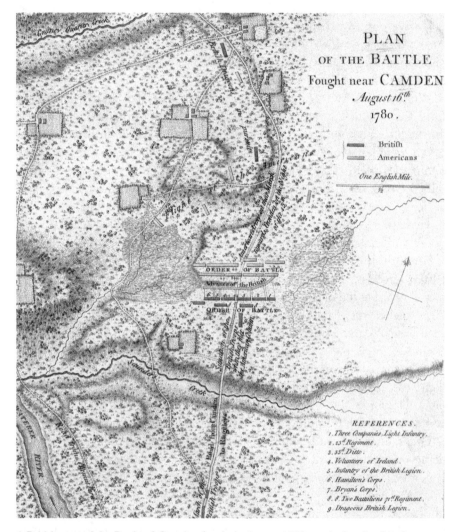

A British map of the Battle of Camden fought in August 1780, made shortly after the engagement. *Library of Congress.*

fired a volley and then steadily advanced with bayonets fixed and struck the Whig militia as the sun came up, routing them with a determined charge "with equal vigour and alacrity on the part of the Troops, who performed everything that can be expected of Men and of Soldiers," an observer reported.[71] Many frightened rebels threw down their muskets without firing a shot while running for the rear "like dastardly cowards," a Continental officer wrote. "General Caswell and myself," reported Gates, "assisted by

The position of General Gates's Marylanders at the Camden battlefield in South Carolina. *Robert Orrison.*

a number of officers did all in our power to rally the broken troops, but to no purpose; for the enemy's cavalry, coming round the left flank of the Maryland Division, completed the rout of the whole of the militia, who left the Continentals alone, to oppose the enemy's whole force." Gates and Caswell were swept from the field trying to reassemble the fleeing troops, which left de Kalb with the Continentals still fighting, along with just one battalion of North Carolina militia that stood fast.[72]

The British then focused their attacks on the Maryland and Delaware troops, the survivors of which also retreated or dispersed into the surrounding swamps, as Tarleton's dragoons pursued the panicked militia along the road toward Charlotte. De Kalb suffered multiple bayonet and gunshot wounds and died in captivity after three days. Meanwhile, Gates, unable to rally the militia, continued riding 180 miles to Hillsborough after a brief respite in Charlotte, "to fall upon some plan, in conjunction with the legislature of this state, for the defense of so much thereof as it is yet possible to save from the enemy." For his perceived three-day "flight" from danger, he was widely criticized in Congress, in newspapers, and by some fellow officers—as well as by historians ever since.[73]

The utter defeat at Camden saw the loss of many captured Continentals, eight artillery pieces, hundreds of muskets, the army's wagon train, and the scattering of hundreds of militiamen. Additionally, with de Kalb's

Monument to General de Kalb in Camden. *Library of Congress.*

death, the American forces lost a capable veteran officer. Coming just three months after the surrender at Charleston and a mere three weeks after Gates had assumed command, this unexpected calamity appeared to be the nadir of American fortunes in the South. Additionally, just two days after Gates's defeat, Tarleton surprised Colonel Thomas Sumter's command of 700 men close to Camden, soundly defeating the Americans at their poorly guarded camp at Fishing Creek along the west side of the Catawba River with only 120 of his dragoons and 40 light infantrymen. Sumter barely managed to escape during the sudden attack, but 300 rebels were captured there.[74]

Gates sent a report to Congress soon after the battle, and the reaction in Philadelphia was demoralizing. The shattering defeat was "a ruinous and destructive" blow to Patriot fortunes in the South, wrote a Maryland delegate, while another lamented "this unfortunate event, [which] at present engrosses the attention of Congress to adopt measures for the defense of the southern states." Samuel Huntington wrote to Gates in early September to advise him of the efforts in Congress to reinforce and supply American forces in the South. Probably expressing the sentiments of most congressmen, Huntington added some encouragement: "[I]t is to be hoped that the panick which it seems had seized the militia will wear off, and that you may yet be able to check the progress of the enemy until more effectual measures may be taken to expel them from South Carolina and Georgia."[75]

Within a few weeks, in fact, the situation in the Carolinas for the Americans did not appear as bleak as it seemed on the evening after the battle. "We have had a severe Rebuke," Gates concluded in an optimistic letter to the French Minister Plenipotentiary to America, the Chevalier de la Luzerne, "but our affairs are by no means desperate…all will be reinstated in this Quarter."[76] Cornwallis did not immediately pursue the frightened rebels beyond several miles north of the battlefield after his victory, nor had the victorious British surged into North Carolina. Cornwallis remained at Camden, resupplying his army and nursing the many wounded soldiers now needing care.

Gates established his headquarters at Hillsborough to reassemble a Patriot army, "from whence and only from whence we can be provided with what is absolutely necessary, for our acting offensively or defensively as occasion shall offer."[77] The itinerant state legislature was also scheduled to meet there in the coming days; in fact, by the end of the month, the assembly had called for all

Samuel Huntington, president of the Continental Congress. *Library of Congress.*

Continental soldiers within the state to rendezvous at Salisbury "to overawe the disaffected in that part of the state." Gates placed additional troops at Salisbury, Guildford Courthouse, and Cross Creek (modern Fayetteville), since not enough supplies had been gathered to allow all his soldiers to remain together. The general advised Washington on August 30 of his situation:

> *I do not think Lord Cornwallis will be able to reap any advantage of consequence, from his victory; as this state seems animated to reinstate and support the army—Virginia I am confident will not be less patriotic. By the joint exertions of the two states, there is good reason to hope, that should the events of the campaign be prosperous to your excellency; all South Carolina might be again recovered.*

Considering that most of his men had to flee the battlefield in panic only two weeks earlier, this showed quite a bit of confidence.[78]

Of course, Gates could not know—nor could anyone else in America at the end of the summer of 1780—that fortune would indeed shine on American arms before all the autumn leaves fell from the trees and that the "Hero of Saratoga" would serve in the Carolinas for only three more months.

Chapter 4

"RESOURCES FEEBLE AND INEFFECTUAL"

The American Army Regroups

Do not gloat over me, my enemy! Though I have fallen, I will rise.
—Michah 7:8

Although General Gates had won the significant American victory at Saratoga three years earlier, and had many supporters in Congress and the army, he recognized after the battle that his tenure as Southern Department commander would soon come to an end. "As unfortunate generals are most commonly recalled," he wrote to General Caswell, "I expect that will be my case, and some other Continental general of rank, sent in my place to command."[79] Several days later, he wrote in a similar vein to General Washington in New Jersey, "If being unfortunate is solely a reason sufficient for removing me from command I shall most cheerfully submit to the orders of Congress; and resign an office few Generals would be anxious to possess."[80]

Negative congressional reaction against Gates was soon expressed once dire news of the battle reached Philadelphia. North Carolina delegate Willie Jones wrote to his governor, Abner Nash, that due to Gates's unmanly conduct, "particularly his rapid retreat, and the length of it…it appears to us that Genl. Gates can no longer continue in that command with satisfaction to himself, or with a prospect of rendering essential service to the United States."[81] John Hanson of Maryland remarked on the "shameful flight of General Gates" and called for his prompt removal. Having led a brigade at Camden, Major General William Smallwood "ought in my opinion take the command of the southern army," wrote Hanson, "or General [Arthur] St. Clair or some other brave officers should supersede Gates."[82] The next week, he again asked that "at least…our runaway general ought to be superseded and an inquiry made into his conduct."[83] Another Maryland delegate suggested an inquiry would be forthcoming, noting also that Washington "probably has, or soon will[,] appoint a successor" to Gates.[84]

By October 5, Congress had determined to proceed with a "Court of Enquiry" of Gates's conduct and to have Washington appoint a successor. Meanwhile, Congressman Mathews of South Carolina wrote to Washington with a recommendation for a new commander: "I am authorized by the delegates of the southern states to communicate to your Excellency their wish that Majr. Genl. Greene may be the officer appointed to command of the Southern Department." Washington offered Greene the command on October 14, and the latter accepted it two days later. This was the genesis of Nathanael Greene's long tenure of command in the southern states, which would last until the end of 1783.[85]

When Congress approved of Washington's decision, Mathews was quite pleased. Greene's appointment, he wrote to the commander-in-chief, "has given general satisfaction to the five southern states. I know it has given the highest satisfaction." Likewise, Nathaniel Peabody of New Hampshire congratulated former Virginia delegate Richard Henry Lee on Greene's new command. "That general's great abilities in the field," Peabody wrote, "his extensive knowledge of the various departments in the army, gives him the advantage of almost every other general officer in America." John Hanson also praised Greene's "experience, prudence and abilities."[86] With this high praise went high expectations for the Rhode Islander as well, as he began his journey southward to assume his new command in the Carolinas.

Still, as a professional soldier, General Gates did not abdicate his command responsibilities after the calamity at Camden, even after receiving word from Congress that he would be replaced by Greene and the subject of an inquiry into his conduct. In fact, he remained active in North Carolina, trying to regroup his army, keeping a watchful eye on the British, and hoping to defend Patriot military stores.

In early September, Gates wrote to Washington about his army's dispositions. "I can only say no considerable alteration has taken place," he began, "the enemy remaining still and the disaffected [Tories] doing nothing of consequence to disturb us." Gates still had to disperse his hungry forces to scattered posts to keep them fed. About 1,400 drafted militiamen from North Carolina were sent to the region around Salisbury

Independence Hall, Philadelphia, meeting place of the Continental Congress. *Library of Congress.*

and Charlotte. Colonel Sumter commanded his own militia force near Charlotte, and he "occasionally acts upon the West Side of the Wateree [River in central South Carolina], and has hitherto given such a jealousy to the British in Camden as to keep them at home." Gates also reported that "three hundred Virginia Riflemen under Colonel [William] Campbell and militia from the back counties are marching to the east bank of the Yadkin [River]," near Salisbury. At Guilford Courthouse, General Stevens brought the Virginia militiamen who had not gone home after Camden, although many were deserting every day. Many of Gates's Maryland Continentals had managed to rally after the battle as well and were with him at Hillsborough with the remaining artillery. The general planned to consolidate the Maryland soldiers "into one strong Regiment, with a good light infantry company," all under Colonel Otho Holland Williams. Gates was also expecting about 500 newly raised and equipped Continentals to join him from Petersburg, Virginia. These regulars, "with the Marylanders above mentioned, will make us stronger in Continental troops than I was before the action," he noted. Gates also hoped that his Continental cavalry units would be equipped at their camps at Halifax—"I hope they will soon be in a condition to obey my orders."[87]

He was also focused on British movements south of Charlotte. In September, he started concentrating his forces at Salisbury, a strategic town where the major road in the Piedmont, the Great Salisbury Road, crossed the wide Yadkin River at Trading Ford, about one hundred miles southwest of Hillsborough. There the militia were led by Brigadier General Jethro Sumner, a capable former Continental officer. Reports from scouts and spies led Gates to conclude that Lord Cornwallis and his army intended to enter North Carolina from the Waxhaws area and march to Charlotte. Taking up a safe position on the east bank of the Yadkin opposite Salisbury, forty-five miles northeast of Charlotte, would allow Patriot forces to watch the enemy's movements, block the key route to the Piedmont, and use the river as a defensive barrier. "You must on no account abandon the defense of that ford," Gates cautioned Sumner, "nor withdraw your guard from the west side of that river until you are, by the near approach of a superior number of the enemy, forced to do it." He ordered General Caswell and the militia he had collected to Salisbury as well.[88]

Despite laborious efforts to strengthen and supply Gates's command, the Continental and state forces at various posts in North Carolina lacked clothes, equipment, serviceable muskets, and just about everything else. Almost all of the army's baggage wagons and supplies had been looted or captured during the ignominious retreat from the Camden battleground, while many of the militia had thrown away their muskets as they ran from the enemy. In the South, muskets were often hard to come by, and there existed few facilities to repair broken, rusted, or poorly maintained weapons. Likewise, artisans and smiths to make shoes, cartridge boxes, belts, swords, cavalry furniture, and other military items were seldom found. Nathanael Greene soon would face the same difficult logistical challenges.

Supply officers in Virginia had great difficulty sending military stores to Gates's army due to a perpetual lack of horse-drawn wagons. Moreover, "the officers and soldiers are in a most wretched situation for want of cloaths of all kinds, particularly shoes and shirts, as also tents, camp kettles, equipage,

Trading Ford on the Yadkin River east of Salisbury. *Author image.*

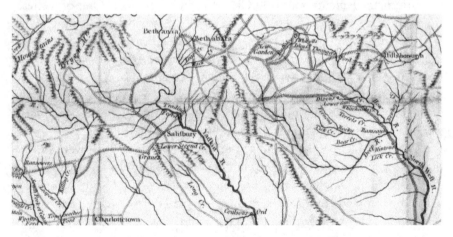

This period map depicts Charlotte (*lower left*), Salisbury (*center*), and Hillsborough (*upper right*), along with the Moravian towns and New Garden area at top. *Library of Congress.*

etc.," wrote Maryland's General Smallwood from Guilford Courthouse on August 31. Some of his soldiers "are mostly barefoot and their feet bruised in such a manner on the route, that several days' rest would be of Service to them," he wrote to Gates. Several weeks later, a militia officer at Guilford reported that the troops "are now quite destitute, without shoe, stocking or blanket, or indeed a possibility of procuring any to protect them from the inclemency of the weather at this sickly season. Some have hardly rags sufficient to cover their nakedness. Add to this that I have no arms to put in their hands." Another officer reported from Ramsey's Mill on the Deep River that the soldiers' "arms [were] in bad order, [and] very short of cartridge boxes....Not a beef secured...[and] no commissary immediately employed to look too for these gross Neglects." Likewise from Hillsborough, Colonel Williams reported the army "being in want of men, magazines, means of transportation, camp equipage, intrenching tools and cloathing, especially blankets and shoes."[89] In one instance, cartridge boxes were in such short supply at Salisbury that the troops made a "substitute...pouch of deer skin & canvas" for their ammunition. This was hardly a force that Gates could use to face Cornwallis's army again.[90]

While Gates and others in North Carolina and Virginia struggled to get the soldiers fed and accoutered, the general continued to receive reports of the British movements south of Charlotte in September. One of Gates's correspondents was Colonel Thomas Polk of Mecklenburg County, who was then in Charlotte, a former Continental officer who served in the Philadelphia Campaign of 1777 and at Valley Forge. In 1780, he led militia forces around Charlotte and served for a time as commissary general for the Salisbury District and commissary of purchase for the army, although a later quarrel with Gates led him to quit both of these roles. Greene would later call him "a man of resource and great influence in the county."[91]

On September 10, Polk reported to Gates that the British were on the march to Charlotte and suggested an attack on Cornwallis's rear. He added that militiamen would engage the enemy column to slow it down, but without reinforcements "I am afraid we are ruined if they come on."[92] The state's General Assembly, then meeting at Hillsborough, became increasingly alarmed at the impending invasion and urged Gates not to withdraw his troops "farther northward":

> *Such a Measure will be productive of the most dangerous, and we apprehend fatal Consequences to this Government, as it will tend to dispirit the Militia and make any efforts from our own internal resources feeble and*

ineffectual; that the good people of this State rest with great Confidence upon the bravery of the Continental Troops and their Commanders, and apprehend that the progress of the British Troops has been retarded from their fears of this respectable body being soon in a capacity to make effectual resistance to them.

The anxious legislators further pledged "that they will exert themselves to obtain an immediate supply of all military and other stores necessary for the Continental Army, and that the utmost strength and credit of this state shall be exerted to make their present station respectable and agreeable to them." In reality, they could hardly help at all.[93]

Another North Carolina militia officer also provided valuable intelligence to Gates from Charlotte. William Lee Davidson, leader of the western militia forces under the overall command of General Sumner, had previously served under Polk in the North Carolina Continental Line, fought at the Battle of Germantown in 1777, and endured the following bitter winter at Valley Forge. After a furlough in 1779 and 1780, Colonel Davidson was left without a command when the Continental troops of North Carolina surrendered at Charleston, so he began serving as second in command of militia forces in the Salisbury District under Brigadier General Griffith Rutherford. Wounded at a victorious battle against Tories at Colson's Mill (near modern Norwood, North Carolina) on July 21, 1780, he missed the Battle of Camden during his recuperation but took the field in late August and was promoted to brigadier general and commander of the Salisbury District after Rutherford was wounded and captured at Gates's defeat.[94]

By the time Cornwallis and the British reached the Waxhaws, Davidson commanded two units of militia on foot. He also counted two mounted companies, led by Mecklenburg's Captain Joseph Graham and former Continental officer Major Joseph Dickson. Also operating in the area was twenty-four-year-old Colonel William Richardson Davie, born in England and reared in the Waxhaws in South Carolina. He graduated from the College of New Jersey (later Princeton University) in 1776 and almost immediately began military service for the Patriot cause. By the time the British were advancing from Camden to Charlotte, Davie had raised a cavalry unit and was providing valuable service to Davidson and Gates.[95]

From a position eight miles south of Charlotte on McAlpine Creek, Davidson advised Gates on September 14 that Cornwallis was still encamped at the Waxhaws, "collecting reinforcements from the Militia, fattening his horse [mounts], and carrying off every article valuable to our Army."

Brigadier General Thomas Sumter commanded South Carolina militia troops supporting Greene's advance operations along the Catawba River. *Library of Congress.*

Thomas Sumter (now a militia brigadier general) and his troops were off to the west on the Catawba River, and General Sumner joined him with more militia from Salisbury a week later. The Whig officers around Charlotte were observing Cornwallis, anticipating his move northward, and concentrating their forces to meet him.[96]

Finally, after almost two weeks of little activity, the dangerous British host was coming at them. "I am to inform you [that] about three o'clock this morning we received information of the enemy's being on their march from the Waxhaws Creek," Sumner wrote to Gates on September 25. "We immediately retreated [to Charlotte], judging it prudent, to prevent, if possible, coming to a Genl. Action" against the British.

North Carolina had finally been invaded.[97]

Chapter 5

"Peace and Quiet to the Country"

Setback to British Conquest

I hate that drum's discordant sound,
Parading round, and round, and round.
To me it talks of ravaged plains,
And burning towns, and ruined swains,
And mangled limbs, and dying groans,
And widow's tears, and orphans' moans;
And all that Misery's hand bestows.
To fill the catalogue of human woes.
—*John Scott of Amwell, "The Drum," 1782*

In the immediate aftermath of his victory near Camden, Lord Cornwallis considered "the rebel forces being at present dispersed" in South Carolina and thus "the internal commotions & insurrections in the province will now subside." Accordingly, he began to plan an offensive into North Carolina. The very day after the battle, he "dispatched proper people into North Carolina with directions to our friends there to take arms & assemble immediately" and to seize "the most violent" Whigs and all their military supplies. Cornwallis promised the Loyalists that he would "march without loss of time" to their support. "Some necessary supplies for the Army are now on their way from Charlestown," he reported to London, "and I hope that their arrival will enable me to move in a few days."[98]

By August 23, Cornwallis had "not yet heard any accounts from No. Carolina" but "hoped that our friends will immediately take arms, as

I have directed them to do." He also desired a possible "diversion in the Chesapeak" conducted by Crown forces from New York that he and Clinton had previously discussed, which would "be of the utmost importance" in distracting American military attention from the Carolinas.[99]

Cornwallis shared his thoughts for the coming move north with Clinton. "It is difficult to form a plan of operations which must depend so much on circumstances," he said, "but it at present appears to me that I should endeavor to get, as soon as possible, to Hillsborough," where he knew American forces were gathering.[100] There Cornwallis wanted to "assemble and try to arrange the friends who are inclined to arm in our favour, and endeavor to form a very large magazine for the winter of flour & meal from the country, and of rum, salt, &c., from Cross Creek" on the Cape Fear River. But these objectives would "depend on the operations which your Excellency [Clinton] may think proper to pursue in the Chesapeak, which appears to me, next to the security of New York, to be one of the most important objects of the war." This was a questionable way to make plans for a campaign into North Carolina. Cornwallis had not heard from Clinton in weeks, did not know Clinton's strategic intentions with any certainty, and could not communicate easily with his superior in distant New York. Coordinating his own maneuvers in the Carolinas with British operations in the Chesapeake would thus be difficult to manage. Given his strained relationship with Clinton, it is not surprising that Cornwallis proceeded with his plans anyway.[101]

After being joined by troops of the 63rd Regiment under Major James Wemyss from Georgetown, South Carolina, Cornwallis readied part of his command to move north from Camden toward Charlotte.[102] His expectations of success were tempered by reports of less than enthusiastic support from Loyalists in North Carolina. "We receive the strongest professions of friendship from North Carolina," he told Clinton, but added that "our friends, however, do not seem inclined to rise until they see our Army in motion." This was another instance of the conundrum British military officers faced since the war began: how to protect the Loyalists after the redcoats left previously "subdued" Whig communities. "The severity of the rebel government has so terrified & totally subdued the minds of the people that it is very difficult to rouze them [Loyalists] to any exertions," Cornwallis reported in frustration.[103] Nevertheless, Cornwallis held out some hope for support of the king. The Loyalists "continue…to give me the strongest assurances of support when His Majesty's Troops shall have penetrated into the interior parts of the Province. The patience and fortitude with which

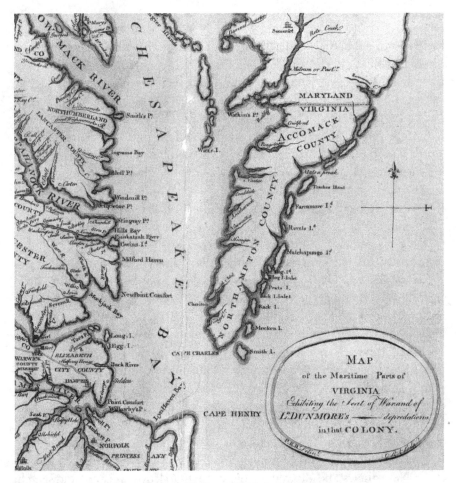

A period map of the lower Chesapeake Bay in Virginia. *Library of Congress.*

they endure the most cruel torments, and suffer the most violent oppressions that a country ever laboured under, convince me that they are sincere, at least as far as their affection to the cause of Great Britain."[104]

In addition to supporting Loyalists, the British also went after the Patriots. Cornwallis reported in late August that "the indefatigable [Thomas] Sumpter is again in the field, & is beating up for recruits with the greatest assiduity."[105] In response, Cornwallis sent Major Wemyss with a mounted detachment to "disarm in the most rigid manner the country between Santee & Peedee" rivers, in the eastern half of South Carolina. They were "to punish severely" the Whigs "who submitted or pretended to live peaceably under His Majesty's government since the reduction of Charlestown" but who subsequently retook the field against the redcoats. The British commander had just ordered Wemyss "to hang up all those militia men" who had recently captured sick soldiers of the 71st Regiment around Cheraw, and at Camden Cornwallis personally "ordered several militia men to be executed, who had voluntarily enrolled themselves and borne arms with us, and afterwards revolted to the enemy." The war in the Carolinas was taking a brutal turn.[106]

By late August, Cornwallis intended to march part of his troops into North Carolina by the second week of September. He planned to reach the Piedmont village of Salisbury by way of Charlotte, to be followed by a subsequent section of his army "about ten days after, with convalescents & stores." He would leave Loyalist troops at Camden "to take care of this place until the sick & stores can be removed." Illness continued to debilitate many of his soldiers: "[O]ur sickness at present is rather at a stand[still], the recoveries nearly keeping pace with the falling down."[107]

Cornwallis wrote to Clinton to remind the commander-in-chief how valuable a diversion in the Chesapeake Bay would be from the British forces at New York or "adding some force to the Carolinas" to bolster his own host. He also reported his newly developed plan to send a sizeable detachment of Tory militia and provincials under the command of Major Ferguson to operate on his left flank as the main army moved north from Camden. "Ferguson is to move into Tryon County [in western North Carolina] with some militia," Cornwallis wrote, "but I am sorry to say that his own experience, as well as that of every other officer, is totally against him." Cornwallis held a low opinion of Loyalist militia units attached to his command and doubted that Ferguson would meet with success in the backcountry west of the Catawba River. Nevertheless, he allowed the detachment to leave his camp and search for armed Whig units to attack in the field.[108]

On September 7, Cornwallis led the veteran 23rd Regiment (the Royal Welch Fusiliers), his own well-drilled 33rd Regiment, the Volunteers of Ireland (an American-raised Loyalist unit), and his field artillery out of Camden to Waxhaws Creek, a staunchly Patriot district south of Charlotte, marching about thirty miles on the east side of the Catawba River.[109] There he was joined by several hundred Loyalist militiamen who had embodied under Colonel Samuel Bryan, most of whom lived on the upper Yadkin River in North Carolina.[110] "Lieut. Col. Tarleton marched the next day with the Light Troops up the west side of the Catawba River," Cornwallis reported on September 19, and the sickly Highlanders of the "71st Regiment, who are beginning a little to recover, are to join me in a few days." Major Wemyss and part of the 63rd Regiment, along with Lieutenant Colonel John

Hamilton's Royal North Carolina Regiment, were left in the Cheraw District of South Carolina "to endeavor to form a militia…on whose fidelity we may place some dependence, and to punish those traitors who, after voluntarily engaging in our militia, deserted to the enemy." Cornwallis expected the 7th Regiment (the Royal Fusiliers) to join him soon and hoped "that nothing can prevent my entering North Carolina before the end of this month."[111]

Still encamped in the forests and fields along Waxhaws Creek on September 22, Cornwallis wrote Clinton a report on his intentions to reclaim the Crown's authority in North Carolina. He would move to Charlotte and "make some redoubts, and to establish a fixed post at that place, and give the command of it to Major Wemyss, whose regiment is so totally demolished by sickness that it will not be fit for actual service for some months." The ambitious general also planned to "bring [to Charlotte] all the sick from Camden who have any chance of being serviceable before Christmas, and trust to opportunities for their joining the army." He sought to make the town a significant base of operations for the redcoats, which suggests his intention of occupying the backcountry for some time. "The post at Charlotte-town will be a great security to all this frontier of South-Carolina, which, even if we were possessed of the greatest part of North Carolina, would be liable to be infested by parties who have retired with their effects over the mountains, and mean to take every opportunity of carrying on a predatory war." He hoped that a western fortified town would "prevent insurrections in this country, which is very disaffected" from the king. Once established at Charlotte, the British would then push northeast to Salisbury on the Yadkin River, "which will open this country sufficiently for us to see what assistance we may really expect from our friends in North-Carolina." It would also "give us a free communication with the Highlanders," who were Loyalists settled at Cross Creek on the Cape Fear River (at modern Fayetteville), "on whom my greatest dependence is placed" for supplies.[112] He hoped too that "upon the appearance of a British army in North Carolina, a great body of the in habitants were ready to join and cooperate with it."[113]

Cornwallis's army was delayed at the Waxhaws by the severe illness of Colonel Tarleton, who was debilitated by fever on September 17 and could not be moved for several days. Tarleton's Legion (without its colonel) finally rejoined the rest of the army on the twenty-third, and by that time, Cornwallis had seen the 71st Regiment's healthy troops and some additional artillery arrive in the British camp.[114]

The British, numbering about 1,200 men, entered North Carolina on September 25, after marching in heavy rain, with Tarleton's Legion in the van commanded by Major George Hanger. Watched from a distance by Captain Graham's mounted Mecklenburg County militia as they advanced, the British reached Charlotte the next day and faced spirited resistance by Colonel Davie's men shooting at them, particularly around the town's courthouse. "For three times we succeeded in repulsing the enemy" dragoon attacks, recalled a Whig veteran of the fight, but "at length we had to yield to superior numbers." A commissary officer serving with Cornwallis wrote that "the whole of the British army was actually kept at bay, for some minutes, by a few mounted Americans," who actually numbered over 100 or more. Apparently, the British Legion was less aggressive in the absence of its leader.[115]

The British remained in Charlotte for several weeks after the skirmish. Cornwallis issued a printed proclamation, distributed to the surrounding countryside, that his army intended to "restore as much peace and quiet to the country as may be possible, during the operations of war," and that

> all those who come into the posts of his Majesty's army under my command, and faithfully deliver up their arms, and give a military parole to remain thenceforth peaceable at home, doing no offence against his Majesty's government, will be protected in their persons and properties, and be paid a just and fair price in gold or silver, for whatever they may furnish for the use of the King's army.

Few Whigs were around to take the oath, however, as some had prudently fled the redcoats' advance, while others doubted that they could be "protected in their persons and properties" if the redcoats later marched away. The region was also known for its predominant Patriot sympathies.[116]

When Cornwallis marched his regiments north to Charlotte, his troops made up the main column of a three-prong advance. As noted earlier, Wemyss led a small force east toward the Pee Dee River to battle Whigs and partisan units among the sluggish rivers and swamps of the Lowcountry, most notably those led by the resourceful Colonel Francis Marion, the famous "Swamp Fox of the Revolution." Far more consequential to Cornwallis's campaign were the frontier operations on the British army's western flank led by Major Ferguson, with a column of more than one thousand Loyalists.

Ferguson was one of several British junior officers who assumed leadership roles of Loyalist units in America for advancement and to receive important commands they would not otherwise have obtained in the regular forces. While senior British officers would not trade their fine scarlet wool coats for the

The difficult mountainous terrain of western North Carolina, across which hundreds of "Overmountain Men" marched to defeat Ferguson's Loyalists at Kings Mountain in 1780. *Library of Congress*.

Loyalists' green regimentals, young men such as Tarleton, Hanger, Rawdon, and John Graves Simcoe grabbed at the notoriety and experience they could achieve commanding active forces on campaign in the colonies. So too did Patrick Ferguson.[117]

Ferguson was a Scotsman born in 1744 and was a regular officer in early years of the Revolutionary War. He also invented a successful breech-loading rifle in 1776 that still bears his name.[118] Wounded at the Battle of Brandywine in 1777, he eventually saw service in the South once promoted to major in the 71st Foot. His appointment as inspector of the Loyalist militia in the Carolinas and Georgia in 1780 gave him the responsibility to organize and train men for active duty against the southern Whigs. Cornwallis never warmed to Ferguson, perhaps because the major was a protégé of Clinton's, whom Cornwallis had grown to detest. Still, he entrusted Ferguson with covering his left flank as he advanced toward North Carolina and recruiting more Loyalists for military service,

The war in the Carolinas, 1780–81. *U.S. Army Center of Military History.*

particularly in sprawling Tryon (later Lincoln) County, North Carolina, west of Charlotte.[119]

As Ferguson marched into the frontier region of the Carolinas, he had to be wary. The month before, just days after the Battle of Camden, frontier Whigs led by Isaac Shelby, James Williams, and Elijah Clark had attacked a Loyalist camp in western South Carolina at Musgrove's Mill, near the Enoree River. There the Tories were soundly defeated on August 19, after which the Americans split up and withdrew. Upon learning of this defeat and that Shelby's column was quickly moving across the mountains into what is now Tennessee, Ferguson aggressively pursued the rebels over increasingly difficult, mountainous terrain. While Cornwallis was at his Waxhaws camp, Ferguson's militia and provincials reached Gilbert Town, a tiny settlement in distant Rutherford County (near today's Rutherfordton).

Meanwhile, General Gates received sporadic intelligence of these distant enemy movements from Patriot officers in Charlotte. "Ferguson, with an Army composed of British & Tories have penetrated into one of the Western Counties of this State," Thomas Polk advised him on September 11, 1780, "and from their mode of march intend to pursue their route through the Frontiers where their party must increase & probably overun some of the interior counties of this district on their return."[120] Likewise, Davidson also reported to Gates. "A Colo. [*sic*] Ferguson in the British service has, by a variety of means, been pernicious to our interest in the west of both the Carolinas," he wrote on October 6, and "there has such a force taken the field against him as will probably rid us of such a troublesome neighbour."[121]

Davidson's prediction proved correct. Alarmed by Ferguson's steady advance and incensed by his inflammatory proclamations, about 1,400 rugged mounted riflemen from western North Carolina, southwest Virginia, and what is now eastern Tennessee rendezvoused in distant frontier valleys and mountain coves before proceeding eastward to confront the impertinent Loyalists' threat. Sensing danger, Ferguson had taken a position on top of the wooded Kings Mountain in South Carolina, thirty miles west of Charlotte, with about 1,000 men, anticipating relief from Cornwallis. There, on October 7, the Whig riflemen surrounded and defeated Ferguson's command, almost all of whom they killed or captured. The Scottish major died in the fighting, and as the 700 prisoners were led away from the battlefield, 9 of the more notorious Tories were hanged from trees along the trail by the "Overmountain Men" after cursory, extra-legal trials. "We fought an hour and five minutes," boasted William Campbell, commander of the Overmountain Men that day, and "the victory was complete to a wish."[122]

Coming just seven weeks after Gates's defeat at Camden, the autumn Battle of Kings Mountain was a serious blow to Cornwallis's plans to invade North Carolina, as well as to Loyalist morale. With the loss of so many of his militia and his western flank now exposed, Cornwallis prudently decided to withdraw his forces from Charlotte beginning on October 12 and retired slowly to Winnsborough, South Carolina, about seventy miles to the south. For the time, North Carolina and Gates's reconstituted army were safe.

Chapter 6

"The Greatest Degree of Anxiety"

Greene Rides South

When thou goest out to battle against thine enemies, and seest horses, and chariots, and a people more than thou, be not afraid of them: for the Lord thy God is with thee, which brought thee out of the land of Egypt.
—Deuteronomy 20:1 (King James Version)

Cornwallis and his soldiers had reached Winnsborough by October 30. The little town was a "healthy spot, well situated to protect the greatest part of the northern frontier, and to assist [the garrisons at] Camden and Ninety-Six," according to the British commander. A small American mounted force under Colonel Davie watched Cornwallis's movements by shadowing the redcoats from the north, as did units led by Sumter, Smallwood, and Brigadier General Daniel Morgan of Virginia, by early November. During the withdrawal, Cornwallis suffered a severe illness that incapacitated him for several weeks. "Had I attempted to penetrate into the further part of N. Carolina," Cornwallis wrote to Major General Alexander Leslie, then leading a diversionary raid in the Chesapeake Bay, "my small Army wou'd have been exposed to the utmost hazard." After the losses at the Battle of Kings Mountain, Cornwallis asked Leslie to bring his troops from the Chesapeake region to the Carolinas to strengthen his army. "We will then give our friends in N. Carolina a fair trial," his Lordship proposed, and if the Loyalists "behave like men it may be of the greatest advantage to the affairs of Britain. If they are as dastardly & pusillanimous as our friends to the southward, we must leave them to their

Cornwallis's headquarters during his army's stay in Winnsborough, 1780–81. *Charles B. Baxley.*

fate & secure what they have got." An air of pessimism and frustration regarding the king's friends had slipped into his correspondence.[123]

Far to the northeast, General Gates made his ragged command ready to march closer to the enemy. Part of his troops left their crude camps at Hillsborough on November 2, bound for Charlotte by way of Guilford Courthouse and Salisbury; Gates himself followed several days later.[124] The marching soldiers, poorly clad and provisioned for late fall maneuvers, eventually reached Charlotte, where Gates set up his headquarters in the courthouse village and posted detachments farther south at New Providence and along Waxhaws Creek, the latter about forty miles from the enemy at Winnsborough. The beleaguered departmental commander also busied himself with the details of arming, equipping, and feeding his army. He sought serviceable "arms[,] accoutrements and rum or cloathing" from Richmond and salt and flour from Petersburg, "or such stores which may be there and more immediately wanting." Gates implored Governor Jefferson "to press Congress to forward all such articles as your state cannot supply. Men merely armed but without cartridges, [cartridge] boxes[,] blankets or tents, are but a poor support to an army." Gates's tired soldiers never did get enough of anything, nor would they for the war's duration.[125]

The first several days in December 1780 were an important time for both armies' commanders situated near the upper reaches of the Catawba River, although no fighting took place between the combatants. At Winnsborough, Cornwallis wrote a long letter to his superior in New York—his first to General Clinton since September 23—reporting his military situation and recent actions. This correspondence, however, offered almost nothing as far as Cornwallis's future plans for operations against the rebels in the Carolinas.

Cornwallis's letter to Clinton, dated December 3, 1780, bemoaned the death of "poor Major Ferguson" at Kings Mountain, where "he was attacked by a very superior force and totally defeated." He also advised Clinton of the American force around Charlotte under Gates and noted that Cornwallis expected Leslie to join him soon with welcomed reinforcements from the Chesapeake Bay. "It will be necessary to drive back the enemy's army, and at the same time to maintain a superiority on both our Flanks," wrote Cornwallis, but he would not "not presume to make Your Excellency any sanguine promises" of success. Still, he did promise "the utmost exertion of my abilities shall be used to employ" expected reinforcements "to the best advantage."[126]

Significantly, Cornwallis also reported that "I am informed that Greene is expected in a few days to relieve Gates."[127] This intelligence, of course, was correct.

Gates also knew that Nathanael Greene was coming to replace him as commander of the Southern Department of the Continental Army. Events would show that this command change would produce a seismic change in the American army's leadership in the South that would soon change the course of the war and ultimately lead to victory for the cause of independence in 1783.

But victory was a long way off when General Greene and a few weary aides rode into Charlotte by way of Salisbury on the afternoon of December 2 and presented Gates a letter from General Washington confirming that the Rhode Islander—fifteen years Gates's junior—would immediately assume command in the South and that Gates was relieved. On the following day, Gates graciously published an order to the troops to announce the momentous change:

The Honorable Major General Greene, who arrived yesterday afternoon in Charlotte, being appointed by His Excellency General Washington, with the approbation of the Honorable the Congress, to the command of the

Southern Army, all orders will, for the future, issue from, and all reports are to be made to, him. General Gates returns his sincere thanks to the Southern Army for their perseverance, fortitude and patient endurance of all the hardships and sufferings they have undergone while under his command. He anxiously hopes their misfortunes will cease herewith, and that victory, with the glory and advantages attending it, may be the future portion of the Southern Army.

In return, Greene thanked Gates publicly on December 5 "for the polite Manner in which he has introduced [Greene] to his Command, and for his good wishes, for the Success of the Southern Army."[128]

Several days later, Gates left Charlotte and made his way home to his lower Shenandoah Valley farm called Traveler's Rest. Although Gates was anxious that a congressionally ordered court of inquiry into his conduct as departmental commander be held immediately, Greene decided that "the circumstances of this army would not admit of the enquiry's being made." Noting that he was "no less desirous of giving you an early opportunity of justifying yourself to the world than you are," Greene sincerely promised

Horatio Gates's home in Virginia's Shenandoah Valley, Traveler's Rest. *Library of Congress.*

his predecessor that as "soon as the state of this army will admit of my convening a Court agreeable to the tenor of my instructions, I will give you immediate notice thereof." In the end, the inquiry was never convened and no charges were brought against Gates, who eventually resumed service with Washington's army late in 1782.[129]

The thirty-eight-year-old officer who succeeded Gates was one of the most remarkable stars in a brilliant constellation of America's Founders, as well as one of the most improbable. Perhaps second only to Washington in strategic competence among Continental officers, Nathanael Greene never won a battle against the British with his own army. In fact, he had no military training or experience prior to the outbreak of hostilities in 1775, save a few months of occasional militia drills. In an age when military bearing and physical strength went a long way toward establishing a general's eminence, Greene had a noticeable limp. Although he fought in numerous major battles and campaigns during the war—including at Brandywine, Germantown, Monmouth Courthouse, Guilford Courthouse, Hobkirk Hill, Ninety Six, and Eutaw Springs—he had been raised in a strong New England Quaker family. While lacking a college education, his erudite wartime correspondence is peppered with humor, political philosophy, classical references, quotes from the Bible and Shakespeare, and literary skill. And while persistently seeking opportunities for battlefield glory and independent command during the first five years of the Revolutionary conflict, Greene reluctantly agreed to serve as Washington's quartermaster general, despite his misgivings. "No body ever heard of a quarter master in history as such or in relating any brilliant action," Greene sullenly wrote to Washington in April 1779. Yet this was the general hand-selected by Washington in the fall of 1780 to restore the prospects of the American cause from Maryland to Georgia.[130]

Greene was born in 1742 into a prominent Rhode Island family in the iron business in Potowomat, Warwick, in Kent County. More interested in educational pursuits than his older brothers, Greene, with his bookish nature, ran into opposition at home. Like many Quakers of that time, his strict father was not supportive of giving his children an extensive formal education. Greene, however, received some tutoring and was well read as a young man. Much of his reading tilted toward military topics by the 1770s. While engaged in the family commercial enterprise, Greene married Catherine "Caty" Littlefield, an attractive orphan of Block Island, in 1774. Soon thereafter, clouds of war covered North America and involved Greene as a militiaman by the end of the year.

Perhaps the least understood period of Greene's life was in early 1775, the beginning of his military career. On June 22, 1775, he received a brigadier general's commission in the newly created Continental Army, the youngest of that rank in the new army, despite little previous military experience to justify such an exalted appointment. He was earlier a mere private for eight months in the Kentish Guards, a Rhode Island militia company founded in 1774. Moreover, he had been passed over by this company when it elected officers in early 1775, much to his embarrassment. Undeterred, he read military manuals and texts voraciously, learned the British army's manual of arms, and continued to drill with the Kentish Guards. Still, it is a mystery as to how Greene received a general's commission so early in the war over several more qualified and politically connected officers.[131]

Few of George Washington's lieutenants saw more active service during the entire war than did Greene. He served under Washington during the Siege of Boston, beginning in the summer of 1775, and then received a major general's commission in August 1776, after the Continental Army shifted its operations to New York to defend that city from an expected British attack. He was ill during the Battle of Long Island on August 27, a

Nathanael Greene Homestead, Coventry, Rhode Island. *Library of Congress.*

Left: Major General Nathanael Greene, American commander of the Southern Department. *Library of Congress.*

Opposite: Fort Washington (*top*) on Manhattan Island was captured by British and Hessian forces in 1776, after Greene advised Washington not to abandon it. *Library of Congress.*

resounding British victory, and his advice to General Washington to defend Fort Washington perched on the Hudson north of the city proved disastrous when the post was lost to the enemy. Nevertheless, the commander-in-chief was still impressed by Greene and continued to rely on him.

Greene continued to serve with Washington's army and ably commanded troops at the Battles of Trenton, Brandywine, and Germantown, all fought in 1777, and at Monmouth Courthouse in 1778. He did yeoman's staff work as well, agreeing to take the army's post as quartermaster general in March 1778. Greene soon brought order and efficiency to the difficult position and earned the sincere thanks of his chief (although his relations with Congress were often contentious). No doubt his quotidian experience running the family's iron business in Rhode Island after his father's death in 1770 contributed to his logistics success, as it also would when he was commander of the Southern Department in the war's last three years.

In July 1780, Greene resigned as quartermaster to resume field command, and Washington later placed him in charge of the strategic American post at West Point after Benedict Arnold's infamous treason there. But he was destined not to serve long by the Hudson, as General Gates had been defeated that summer in the piney woods near Camden and a new American commander was now needed in the Southern Department. Washington chose Greene for the job.[132]

Washington officially appointed Greene to the command of the Southern Department on October 22 from the main army's encampment in New Jersey. Greene was to "proceed without delay" to the Carolinas. Washington also assigned the troops of the Virginia-born, twenty-four-year-old Major

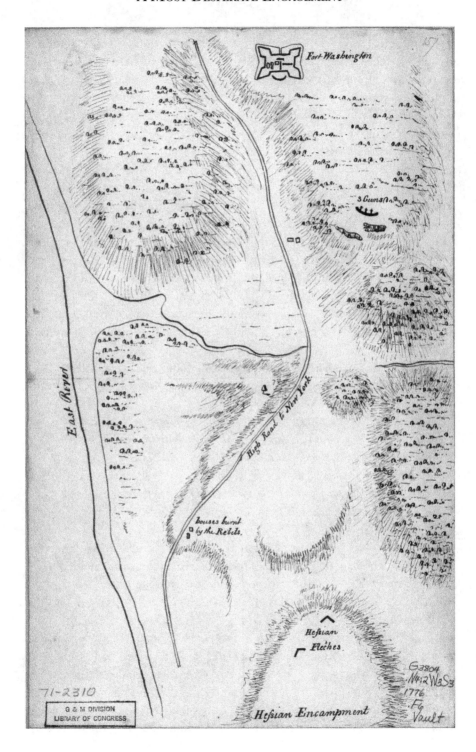

Henry "Light-Horse Harry" Lee to the southern theater to help ensure Greene's success. The brash Lee, soon promoted to lieutenant colonel, would become Greene's most trusted lieutenant and performed superbly in battle and on the march. In addition, Greene would be accompanied by Major General Baron von Steuben, the Continental Army's former drill master at Valley Forge, inspector general, and now Greene's chief assistant to rebuild American forces in the South.

By October 27, Greene had reached Philadelphia, where he met with Congress and tried to secure money and logistical support for his new command.[133] Several of Greene's letters from Philadelphia show that he learned there that rebuilding an effective army in the South would be daunting. "The army exists more in name than in substance," he wrote, and he ruefully guessed "that the American cause is at death's door." Greene had heard of the pitiable condition of the troops in the Carolinas, who were in the "greatest distress imaginable," but "Congress are by no means alarmed at their critical situation." The ordnance department was "in a wretched deranged state," and the southern army in general "has only an imaginary existence."[134]

To Washington, Greene wrote a despairing letter outlining the problems he faced even before arriving at his new command:

> *Nothing is expected from* [the troops] *unless large supplies can be forwarded from the Northward. They are altogether without clothing and blankets, and totally unfit for any kind of service. To carry them into the field in this condition will only fill the hospitals and sacrifice the lives of a great many valuable men. Arms are not less wanting than clothing, and wagons as much as either.*

His military prospects were "dismal, and truly distressing." He grew frustrated at the lack of financial support he received from private parties in the city as well. "If there is not public spirit enough in the people to defend their liberties, they well deserve to be slaves," he observed, not for the last time.[135]

Continuing his long journey on November 4, Greene was accompanied by his trusted aides Major Ichabod Burnet of New Jersey and Lieutenant Colonel Lewis Morris Jr., a Bronx native, veteran of many of the army's major battles, and Greene's aide since 1779. They rode south along the Chesapeake to Annapolis, where Greene met with Maryland state leaders to obtain support for his troops, hundreds of whom were Continentals from

STATE HOUSE
. Annapolis Md

General Greene visited the Maryland legislature at Annapolis in 1780 to secure supplies and reinforcements for his southern army. *Library of Congress.*

that state. There he learned from political figures and military officers that his prospects for obtaining arms, money, and supplies grew less likely the farther south he traveled. A Maryland army officer advised him that unless supplies were procured in the North and transported to the southern states, "it is idle to expect service" from the army. Without immediate and adequate support, he wrote to Maryland's governor Thomas S. Lee, "I see myself devoted to ruin and the Southern States to subjection."[136]

Greene, von Steuben, and staff crossed the wide Potomac River at Alexandria, Virginia, and stopped for one night at Mount Vernon to visit with Martha Washington, the general's wife. From the Washingtons' impressive riverside plantation home, the traveling officers proceeded south on rough roads by way of Colchester, Dumfries, Fredericksburg, and Hanover Court House before arriving at Richmond, Virginia's new state capital, on November 16.[137] Along the way, Greene tried to determine if clothing and other supplies could be had in Virginia but was disappointed. At Richmond, he found matters "in the greatest state of confusion," he reported to Washington, particularly since a large British force under General Leslie had been raiding the state's Tidewater region almost unimpeded over the last several weeks. Money was scarce, recruits were few and ill equipped, and the lack of wagons and horses meant that supplies could not be moved easily to the Carolinas. In fact, the need for proper transportation was so great that he began to explore the possible use of rivers in Virginia and North Carolina to ship supplies and weapons by boat. "Provisions and forage are plenty in the country if we can but hit upon measures to collect and convey them to the Army," he observed. Still, the near chaotic conditions in the South worried him: "I cannot contemplate my own situation without the greatest degree of anxiety."[138]

Here at Richmond, Greene began to develop a relationship with Governor Jefferson, who would remain in office until June 2, 1781. Virginia was expected to provide much of the supplies, firelocks, powder, equipment, horses, and wagons for the war effort in the South, as the British had overrun South Carolina after the Battle of Camden, and the much poorer North Carolina lost most of its dearly procured military resources in the bloody debacle. Although Jefferson's wartime performance as his state's chief executive would soon become controversial—and would remain so for decades—his constant efforts to defend his beloved Virginia during several devastating British incursions dating back to 1779 were hampered by a lack of men and materiel, constitutional limits on gubernatorial authority, and the enemy's maritime superiority on Virginia's numerous rivers, inlets, bays, and coast. Nevertheless, Jefferson worked hard to sustain Greene's army.[139]

While in tiny Richmond, Greene urged Jefferson to redouble efforts to provide for his upcoming campaign in the Carolinas. The general needed "timely support," including well-equipped militia companies to augment his Continentals, along with stores of food and depots to repair arms. No doubt many private conversations took place along the James River capital in which Virginia's political officials and military officers regretfully informed the Rhode Island general how little they had to provide or purchase. Sensing the critical need for a determined facilitator of men and materiel to be sent south, Greene left Baron von Steuben in Virginia while he continued onward to his new command.[140]

Traveling by way of the old tobacco port town of Petersburg on the Appomattox River, Greene rode southwest and entered North Carolina by November 26. After staying at the home of well-known Patriot Thomas Person,

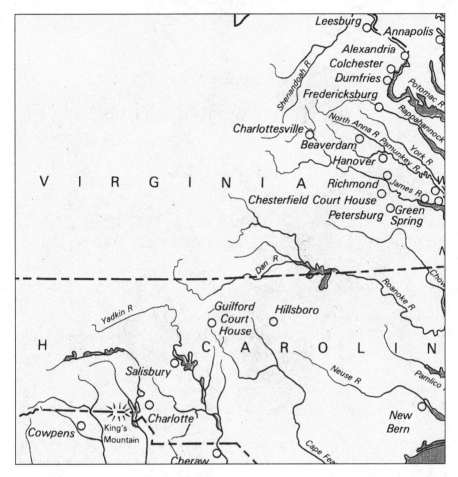

The area of Greene's route south to assume his new command, taking him through Virginia and North Carolina. *U.S. Army Center of Military History.*

he reached Hillsborough the following day, but General Gates had just left the rustic town to go to Charlotte, where the army was posted. At Hillsborough, Greene observed that although they had performed little service, the large number of militia troops mobilized from the Carolinas and Virginia since the summer had consumed vast quantities of supplies, which made the sustainment of the Continental troops at Charlotte far more difficult. With no time to waste, the Rhode Islander proceeded to the crossroads village of Salisbury and arrived at army headquarters in Charlotte on December 2.

Chapter 7

"THE SHADOW OF AN ARMY"

Preparing for Victory

*The truly great leader overcomes all difficulties....The lack of equipment, the
lack of food, the lack of this or that are only excuses; the real leader displays this
quality in his triumphs over adversity, however great it may be.*
—*General George C. Marshall, 1941*

When General Greene rode into the southern army's rude encampment
at Charlotte on December 2, he was astounded at what he found.
As the editors of Greene's modern published papers wrote, "while Greene
had known that the Southern Army lacked most of the essentials needed
by troops in the field, he was scarcely prepared for the appalling conditions
he encountered" when assuming the command.[141] After meeting with
General Gates and other officers at headquarters, Greene inspected the
ragged soldiers, their squalid camps, and the army's meager supplies. He
saw pitiable, shoeless soldiers without uniforms and food, bare-bone horses
pulling old wagons and cannons, and sickness among the thin ranks. "I find
nothing but the shadow of an army in the midst of distress,"[142] he wrote
desperately to Governor Abner Nash of North Carolina a few days later, in
a letter typical of many he penned in his first days in North Carolina.

To Governor Jefferson he described the alarming scene:

> *I find the troops...in a most wretched condition, destitute of every thing
> necessary either for the comfort or convenience of soldiers. It is impossible
> that men can render any service...whilst they are starving with cold and*

hunger. Your [Virginia] *troops may be literally said to be naked and I shall be obliged to send a considerable number of them away into some secure place and warm quarters until they can be furnished with clothing. It will answer no good purpose to send men here in such a condition, for they are nothing but added weight upon the army, and altogether incapable of aiding in its operations....The life of a soldier in its best state is subject to innumerable hardships, but when they are aggravated by a want of provisions clothing, his condition becomes intolerable, nor can men long contend with such complicated difficulties and distress—deaths, desertion and the hospital must soon swallow up an army under such circumstances.*[143]

Greene went on to lecture Jefferson that "you raise men in vain unless you clothe, arm and equip them properly for the field." Moreover, the destitute troops were without tents, and food was obtained precariously by daily collections in the neighborhood of the soldiers' camps rather than supplied regularly by depots.[144]

To the North Carolina Board of War, a recently created committee tasked with overseeing the state's military efforts, Greene reminded it that "it was said by a certain general that in order to have a good army you must begin by providing well for the belly, for that is the mainspring of every operation." The beleaguered board, of course, was well aware of the army's staggering logistical woes, as General Gates had also implored it repeatedly to aid his suffering troops while he commanded the Southern Department.[145]

The state, however, could do little to help the pitiable soldiers. After the twin debacles at Charleston and Camden in 1780—where so many of North Carolina's troops, firearms, wagons, and precious military equipment were lost—there was little the state could provide or purchase for the army. "All the funds of this State have been exhausted in the course of the late campaign," Governor Nash lamented in the fall, "the horses, wagons, tents, arms, camp equipage of every kind, the pay and bounty of the militia, and the provision of beef, pork, flour, spirits, sugar, coffee, wine, medicines, etc., etc., all fell upon us, besides the payment of very large sums on Congress[ional] draughts, & all was lost in a single hour" at Camden.[146]

Perhaps seeking to commiserate with those closest to him in spirit, Greene wrote two private letters on the seventh to distant correspondents explaining the daunting challenges he encountered. To his wife back in Rhode Island he described the army as "nothing but a few half-starved soldiers who are remarkable for nothing but poverty and distress."[147] And to General Washington in New Jersey he said that "nothing could be more wretched and distressing than the condition of the troops, starving with cold and hunger...those of the Virginia line are literally naked, and a great part totally unfit for any kind of duty."[148]

Likewise, one of Greene's soldiers in this period recalled that "at this time the troops were in a most shocking condition for the want of clothing, especially shoes, and we having kept open campaign all winter the troops were taking sick fast." Indeed, by the end of the month, Greene's own assessment had grown even bleaker. "The small force that I have remaining with me are so naked & destitute of every thing, that the greater part is rendered unfit for any active kind of duty," even drill or parades. Conceptual images and illustrations many modern readers, artists, and authors have of numerous well-fed, armed Continental soldiers smartly turned out in new blue wool regimentals clearly do not depict the southern army Greene inherited at the end of 1780.[149]

Given the critical needs of his bedraggled troops, Greene dived into the innumerable tasks at hand to put his army on a proper footing. His previous experience as Washington's quartermaster general was invaluable to American fortunes in the South at this point. In fact, Greene began his thankless efforts to supply the army even before he arrived at headquarters. From Salisbury on his journey south from Richmond, he wrote to General Stevens in Virginia about meeting the army's logistical needs. Greene believed that "the Yadkin [River, in North Carolina's Piedmont] may be made subservient to the business of transportation of stores from Virginia." He ordered a party of soldiers to scout the river in December to assess its logistical usefulness and judge if this water course could accommodate "boats of a peculiar kind" called bateaux. This method of transport would be less expensive than land transportation, although numerous wooden boats would have to be built. "There will be difficulties," Greene conceded, "but I hope not insurmountable." Later, he wrote to Jefferson, "[I]f this plan succeeds I am in great hope of receiving very considerable supplies from Virginia."[150]

Only one day after assuming command, Greene ordered others to explore the Catawba, Dan, and Roanoke Rivers for the same purpose. All of these tireless officers, including the inestimable Polish-born engineer Colonel Thaddeus Kosciuszko, were also to observe the conditions and locations of nearby roads and fords, as far down as Taylor's Ferry on the Roanoke River, in Virginia. Governor Jefferson had tried to establish a waterborne transportation network earlier in the year, and Greene was no doubt informed of the scheme by Colonel Edward Carrington, a young Virginian of

The Polish-born Thaddeus Kosciuszko, Greene's valuable chief engineer, served in the army's Southern Department. *Library of Congress.*

remarkable administrative talents whom Greene appointed deputy quartermaster general for the southern army.[151] The thirty-two-year-old Carrington was a former artillery officer, and although he lacked any previous quartermaster experience, his innate abilities proved equal to the task.[152]

The Rhode Island general sent out a flurry of letters from Charlotte to reinvigorate his army's dilapidated supply system. To the North Carolina Board of War, he asked for the establishment of magazines and supply depots in the state, for beef and salt pork, more wagons, for a month's provisions to be collected at Charlotte, for rum, and for salt—"a capital article." He ordered tents to be made out of sailcloth and cotton duck on hand, as he saw no shelters in the soldiers' camps. He asked for smith and carpenter tools, files, and crosscut saws. He ordered supplies from the eastern part of the state, not threatened with an imminent enemy invasion, to be transferred immediately to his camps at Charlotte. Many of these sought-after items were to be purchased if possible but confiscated for public use if not. "It gives me pain to be obliged to take private property, either contrary to law or the consent of the owners," he regretted in January 1781, but "remote evils must be submitted to, to prevent immediate misfortune," meaning the dispersal of his army.[153]

Greene, of course, met many officers in the department at Charlotte and in the weeks to come and made good use of them. Colonel Nicholas Long of Halifax, the long-serving deputy quartermaster for North Carolina, retained his congressionally appointed position.[154] Greene also asked Colonel Davie to assume the role of the department's commissary general, "of great consequence to the Army; and all our future operations depend on it." The twenty-five-year-old Davie reluctantly accepted the position and served in that role until May 1781. He had seen much active service in the Carolinas—including a battle wound at Stono Ferry, South Carolina, in 1779. As noted earlier, he also led mounted militia troops against the British at Charlotte in September 1780.[155]

One of the most important figures Greene encountered at Charlotte was Colonel Otho Holland Williams, former commander of the 6th Maryland Regiment, who had seen action at Fort Washington, New York, in 1776 (where he was captured), the Battle of Monmouth in 1778, and during the brief Camden Campaign, in which he served as Gates's deputy adjutant general. Greene kept Williams in that post initially, but Williams also commanded Maryland troops in the South after the state's decimated regiments were consolidated prior to Greene's arrival in the Carolinas. Williams would render outstanding service to American arms in the months to come.[156]

No doubt the most colorful character Greene saw at his Charlotte headquarters was Daniel Morgan from the lower Shenandoah Valley, a hard-fighting, gritty officer of extensive Continental service and a tough veteran of the French and Indian War (including Braddock's campaign) and Dunmore's War in 1774. Born in 1736, Morgan led two rowdy Virginia rifle companies during the Siege of Boston in 1775, followed by a grueling, ultimately disastrous expedition against Quebec under Benedict Arnold at the end of the same year. Taken prisoner in Canada, Morgan was exchanged in 1776. Promoted to colonel, he led a large contingent of riflemen during the Saratoga Campaign in 1777, in which he significantly contributed to Gates's crucial victory there. After the harsh 1777–78 winter at Valley Forge with Washington's army, Morgan's men engaged in the pursuit of the British after the Battle of Monmouth. Insulted at not being promoted to command the army's light infantry brigade in 1779, he resigned his commission in protest; however, upon learning of the 1780 defeat at Camden, Morgan's patriotism led him to rejoin the army and reach Gates's camps at Hillsborough in September. He was promoted to brigadier general the following month and given command of Gates's newly formed light troops. Greene kept him in this role, for which Morgan was exceptionally well suited. He would soon demonstrate a penchant for independent leadership as well.[157]

Greene's soldiers numbered between 2,300 and 2,500 men when he assumed command, although only about 1,500 were present in the ranks. The rest were sick, on detached duty, or absent without leave. He counted more than 900 ill-clad Continental troops in the depleted Maryland and Delaware regiments, fewer than 100 poorly furnished Continental light dragoons, and a company of Virginia Continentals. Most of these soldiers were long-serving regulars led by experienced officers, and many had fought at Camden, where their ranks had been thinned as a result of that defeat.

Lieutenant Colonel John Eager Howard was a distinguished Maryland Continental officer who fought at Guilford Courthouse. *Library of Congress.*

In the late fall, Gates had divided his army by placing under General Morgan a light force (or "flying army") consisting of 70 Continental Light Dragoons under William Washington, a second cousin of the commander-in-chief, a former seminarian from Stafford County, Virginia, and a "thunderbolt of war," according to a North Carolina militiaman; 60 Virginia riflemen; hundreds of North Carolina and Virginia militiamen; and a detachment of Continentals made up of about 320 Maryland and Delaware troops commanded by Lieutenant Colonel John Eager Howard, a competent twenty-eight-year-old Baltimore native. General Greene thought so well of Howard that he later wrote the young Marylander "deserves a statue of gold." Within weeks, South Carolina and Georgia militia also joined Morgan's wing.[158]

The rest of Greene's Maryland regulars were commanded by Colonel Otho Holland Williams. The elite, mixed unit of infantry and cavalry called Lee's Legion—the "bedrock" of the army, wrote one historian—reinforced the army in late January. It's commander, Lieutenant Colonel Henry "Light-Horse Harry" Lee, was of a leading Virginia family, a brash officer who would soon show his considerable military initiative and endurance in the coming campaign. The balance of Greene's main army consisted of hundreds of state troops and militia forces called up for duty with the army from Virginia and North Carolina, whose numbers fluctuated almost day to day.[159]

The use of militia troops by Americans during the Revolutionary War was often seen by military officers and politicians as a necessary evil. The letters and reports of many Revolutionary War leaders are full of uncomplimentary assessments of militia forces. One North Carolina general wrote in 1779 that the militia "when embodied are in such a naked, defenceless state that they have but a feint resemblance to a military force" and that they turned out "badly armed, and entirely without the necessary Equipment." General Greene learned that in the Carolinas, "the Militia are calculated to destroy provisions [rather] than oppose the Enemy." Even as early as 1776, Greene expressed his dislike of using temporary soldiers:

People coming from home with all the tender feelings of domestic life are not sufficiently fortified with natural courage to stand the shocking scenes of war. To march over dead men, to hear without concern the groans of the wounded, I say few men can stand such scenes unless steeled by habit or fortified by military pride.

Just before his appointment to the southern command, he wrote that "there are a thousand disadvantages which spring from the mode of employing militia," the reliance on which could only result in "fatal effects." While "at first it may afford a seeming security," dependence on the militia to fight the enemy actually just wasted the South's limited resources. Gates's Camden defeat convinced Greene that "surely we have had enough to convince us that the liberties of America ought not to be trusted in the hands of the Militia."[160]

As Greene soon came to learn, however, officers charged with securing American independence had little choice other than to employ the militia in their departments. On one hand, militiamen won notable Patriot victories at Concord, Massachusetts; Oriskany, New York; and Kings Mountain, noted earlier. They also contributed substantially to American successes in the Saratoga and Yorktown Campaigns. Yet too often they were unreliable, expensive to maintain in the field, and consumed valuable resources for service of only limited duration. Often they deserted in droves without shame, taking their army-issued flintlocks with them. At times they fled in the face of an enemy assault without staying to fire a single shot. The southern states, however, had to rely on the militia for defense, in part due to their inability to raise Continental troops for extended periods of time. However, this heavy reliance on militia forces in the southern theater of the war greatly contributed to the chaos so rampant in Carolinas during the struggle for independence. Nevertheless, while civil and military leaders in the South complained about the numerous and glaring shortcomings of the militia, they were obliged to rely on this problematic class of soldiery for much of their strength and support.

Greene's strategy once in command in the South was one of caution and patience. In part this was dictated by the wretched condition of his army, the major logistical problems he and his staff were trying to correct, and a recognition of political factors. "My great object will be, to avoid a great misfortune," he wrote in December 1780, recognizing that he needed to keep an army in the field to shore up the Whigs' morale and fortitude. Moreover, he did not want to repeat the mistakes of Lincoln at

Savannah and Charleston and Gates at Camden.[161] "It appears to me," Greene wrote, "the misfortunes of this quarter [i.e., the southern theater] have been owing to the [previous] commanding officers putting too much to the hazard and this I fear with a view of complying with the wishes and impatience of the inhabitants." He concluded that the "ill judged exertions" of his Continental Army predecessors "only serve to fix the chains so much faster" after battlefield defeats. To the North Carolina Board of War, he wrote that "while so much depends upon the opinion of the people both as to men and money, as little should be put to the hazard as possible." The army should be "employed in the partisan [irregular] way until we have a more permanent force...if we put things to the hazard in our infant state before we have gathered sufficient strength to act with spirit and activity and meet a second misfortune all may be lost."[162] Writing in a similar vein to South Carolina's most famous partisan officer only two days after taking command, he told Francis Marion that "until a more permanent Army can be collected than is in the field at present we must endeavor to keep up a partizan war and preserve the tide of sentiment among the people as much as possible in our favor."[163]

It would be just over three months after his arrival at Charlotte before Greene would "put things to the hazard," but in the meantime, he had to make immediate strategic and logistical decisions in the face of the enemy, who would soon be on the move into North Carolina once again.

Chapter 8

"A COMPLETE VICTORY"

The Battle of Cowpens

...O now, who will behold
The royal captain of this ruined band
Walking from watch to watch, from tent to tent,
Let him cry, "Praise and glory on his head!"
For forth he goes, and visits all his host,
Bids them good morrow with a modest smile,
And calls them brothers, friends, and countrymen.
—William Shakespeare, Henry V, *Act 4, Prologue*

Less than a week after his arrival at Charlotte, General Greene began to prepare to move part of his army south to a site on the Pee Dee River in South Carolina, but he kept Morgan's "Flying Army" west of the Catawba River, closer to Cornwallis's position at Winnsborough. Feeding his troops was his chief concern. "The subsistence of this army," Greene wrote to the North Carolina Board of War on December 14, "is so precarious and difficult to obtain...that I am not a little alarmed for its existence. We are now fed with great difficulty by daily collections, and the prospects grow more and more unpromising." He lamented that "in the present state of things it is almost impossible to carry on any offensive operations."[164]

Greene expected Morgan's mostly mounted detachment to be engaged in operations in South Carolina with militia reinforcements from Sumter, Davidson, and Elijah Clarke, a partisan commander from Georgia, to threaten British outposts and "spirit up the people." Meanwhile, Greene moved the rest of his troops to a "camp of repose" at Hicks Creek in the Cheraws area of South Carolina, a healthier environment perhaps better suited to obtaining supplies. This site was chosen by Colonel Kosciuszko across (east of) the Pee Dee River from Cheraw Hill and would allow Greene to refit and discipline the troops into a fighting force, albeit a small one "destitute of everything." General Stevens of the Virginia militia was also in camp but had "not the smallest glimpse of hope left of doing anything in that way with those men who are here under my immediate command, as their times are just about expiring, and I am ordered to march in the morning to take charge of the prisoners and conduct them to Virginia." Likewise, the officers were "recruiting the troops," Greene's aide Major Burnet wrote from the camp, "but are destitute of clothing and stores of every kind. The staff departments are entirely deranged…the troops under Green have almost worn out their Clothing—we get but about half our allowance of meal, but hope for a better supply in the future." Greene hoped that the movement into South Carolina would be perceived by the Patriot inhabitants of the Carolinas as an advance and thus bolster their morale. His troops, fewer than eight hundred of whom were uniformed and fit for duty, reached the Hicks Creek site on the day after Christmas 1780.[165]

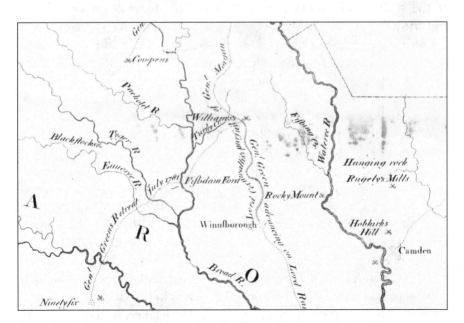

Upper South Carolina map depicting Camden, Ninety Six, Cowpens, and Winnsborough. *Library of Congress.*

While Greene feared splitting his small army into two locations, he had little choice due to logistical constraints. This audacious move, however, was strategically quite risky. It would put the two sections of his command about 120 miles apart and leave his troops vulnerable if attacked by the superior forces of the British, who were between the two American camps. If the enemy moved fast enough, they could attack and defeat the troops of Morgan and Greene separately and then swiftly march in to conquer North Carolina. As historians George Scheer and Hugh Rankin observed, Greene was "defying the classic injunction of warfare that to divide an inferior force in the face of a superior army was to invite the enemy to destroy first one then the other of the parts." The Continental general, however, gambled that the risk was worth taking. A few days after arriving at the Cheraws camp, he was "well-satisfied with the movement, for it has answered thus far all the purposes from which I intended it. It makes the most of my inferior force, for it compels my adversary to divide his, and holds him in doubt as to his own line of conduct."[166]

To the west along the Catawba, Morgan's advance into South Carolina threatened one of the key British fortified bases in the backcountry, Ninety Six, possession of which allowed the redcoats and Loyalists to control much of the state's backcountry region. To counter Morgan's growing threat and crush the smaller American force separated from Greene's main army, Cornwallis dispatched Colonel Tarleton with his Legion, the 1st Battalion of the 71st Regiment, and the 7th Regiment of Foot "to push him [Morgan] to the utmost" and defend Ninety Six. Moving swiftly, Tarleton's 1,100 men were able to block Morgan's threat to the backcountry and then turn on the American force. Meanwhile, Cornwallis planned to advance his own troops from Winnsborough and once again enter North Carolina near Charlotte.[167]

Aware of the enemy's aggressive movements, Morgan wisely retreated northward in cold, rainy weather, supplying his army by confiscating Tory-owned supplies, muskets, and gunpowder along his route. Driving his men hard, Tarleton chased the weary American soldiers until he got within striking range on the night of January 16–17, near Morgan's position just south of the Broad River in an open grassland called the Cowpens. There, aided by a humorless South Carolina militia general named Andrew Pickens, Morgan decided to make a stand and arranged his troops to take advantage of their strengths. He deployed militia skirmishers in his first line, with orders to fire two volleys at the approaching enemy and then fall back to a second line of Georgia and South Carolina militiamen when pressed. These second line

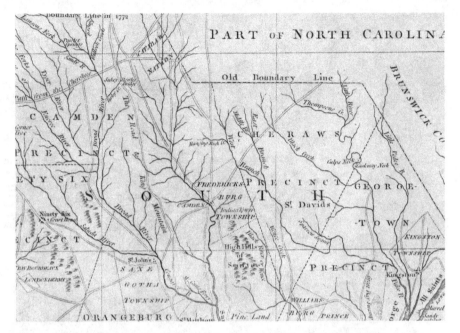

Upcountry South Carolina, depicting Camden (*center*) and Ninety Six (*left*). *Library of Congress.*

troops would also fall back after firing several volleys, reforming behind a third line of Continental infantry on an open rise, supported by Colonel Washington's mounted, white-coated dragoons.

The wily Morgan was taking a valuable lesson from Gates's faulty deployment of his undependable militia forces at Camden; Morgan instead placed his own militia companies in the front two lines and only tasked them with limited duty—firing at least a few rounds to delay and bloody the advancing enemy and then falling back to a safe position behind the steadfast regulars. Perhaps Morgan's most effective preparation for battle was mingling with his anxious soldiers around their fires the evening beforehand, confidently explaining his plan, encouraging the men, and showing a stalwart command presence. An old veteran himself, he knew how to steady his troops.[168]

Morgan's plan worked like a charm. Tarleton deployed his men impetuously, "shouting as they advanced," and attacked head on at dawn before all his troops were ready to make the assault. Standing in a wet field at sunrise, the nervous rebel militia fired as told, Morgan's steady Continentals held their ground, and Colonel Washington's dragoons made a terrific charge into the British ranks, almost annihilating

Cavalry action at the Battle of Cowpens. *U.S. Army National Guard Bureau.*

Tarleton's detachment. The Legion commander was fortunate to escape the battleground with several dozen remaining dragoons and hurried east for the safety of Cornwallis's camps by Turkey Creek thirty miles away, pursued partway by Washington's cavalry. The British lost about six hundred soldiers as prisoners and suffered more than one hundred killed—a staggering loss on the eve of Cornwallis's invasion of North Carolina. Cowpens was one of the most clear-cut triumphs for Americans during the war, "a complete victory" Morgan proudly reported to Greene two days later, in which the Americans also captured two enemy cannons. Greene wrote that "the victory was compleat, and the action glorious. The brilliancy and success with which it was fought, does the highest honor to the American arms and adds splendor to the character of the General and his officers." To Cornwallis, now deprived of a quarter of his army, this "unfortunate affair…was a very unexpected and severe blow."[169] To Lord Rawdon, he wrote on January 21 that "the late affair has almost broke my heart," but he vowed to chase Morgan, who marched quickly northward with his prisoners to the Catawba River immediately after his victory.[170]

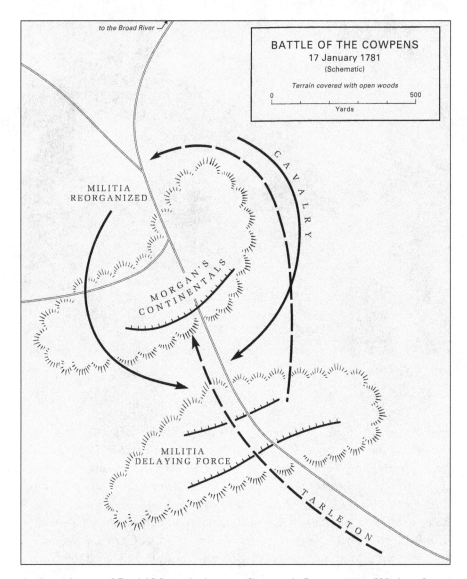

A schematic map of Daniel Morgan's victory at Cowpens in January 1781. *U.S. Army Center of Military History.*

In South Carolina, the British commander worked on a plan. Even before the Battle of Cowpens, Cornwallis had written on January 6 to his superior, General Clinton, of his intentions to advance northward "on the west side of the Catawba for a considerable distance…then proceed to pass that river and the Yadkin. Events alone can decide the future steps."[171] Cornwallis was

At Ramsour's Mill, Cornwallis ordered all of his army's excess baggage burned prior to chasing Greene to the Dan River. *Jeffrey P. Oves.*

finally ready to move. With reinforcements received on January 18 from General Leslie by way of Charleston, he now commanded 2,800 soldiers serving in the 23rd, 33rd, and 71st Regiments; a large amalgamated brigade of companies of the three elite British Guards regiments led by the popular Brigadier General Charles O'Hara; the blue-coated Hessian Regiment von Bose; a company of rifle-bearing Jaegers (Hessian light infantry); Tarleton's British Legion; and Colonel Hamilton's Royal North Carolina Regiment, a Loyalist unit. Morgan's victory at Cowpens, however, reduced the British force considerably.[172]

On January 19, just two days after Tarleton's defeat, Cornwallis and his host set out after Morgan, who was then at Gilbert Town in the backcountry about seventy miles west of Charlotte. Morgan was moving rapidly east in rainy weather and crossed the Catawba River at Sherrald's (Sherrill's) Ford, twenty-five miles north of Charlotte, after he sent the hundreds of Cowpens captives farther north toward Virginia. A militiaman recalled that "after the battle the troops suffered greatly on their return to Salisbury…with the [British] prisoners [and] from the high waters [in the rivers,] cold rains and want of provisions." Once safe from the British for the time being on the east side of the rising river, Morgan halted his troops and deployed them to guard the many Catawba crossings.[173]

Cornwallis and his army camped at Ramsour's Mill on January 25, near the South Fork of the Catawba (at modern Lincolnton). "Morgan's movements have been too rapid for me," he wrote to Lord Rawdon that day, "and he has passed the Catawba," ten miles away. "My situation is most critical." Cornwallis worried that advancing could be dangerous, "but certain in retreating. I am therefore determined to go on," despite moving farther away from his base of supplies with each step. Then he took a radical decision. Since the army's wagons and baggage slowed its progress,

Major General Nathanael Greene of Rhode Island. *Library of Congress.*

Cornwallis "determined to burn all my wagons except those loaded with rum, salt, spare ammunition and hospital stores." An observer with the Crown forces noted that the general destroyed his own superfluous property first, setting an extraordinary example "that was cheerfully followed" by the other officers, who consigned much of their personal luxuries to the flames. The weary men in the ranks also submitted to this hardship, though perhaps with less zeal, even as the rum was destroyed. Cornwallis reported to Rawdon that his men were "healthy and full of zeal."[174] More enthusiastically, General O'Hara wrote that they were in "a barren, inhospitable, unhealthy part of North America," but "it was resolved to follow Greene's army to the end of the world."[175]

The British left Ramsour's Mill on January 28. The next day, they reached Beattie's Ford, a few miles downstream of Sherrald's Ford, but the Catawba River was too high to cross due to the incessant rains that month. "When the American troops reached the north bank of the Catawba, the British army was on the south bank of the same stream," a rebel soldier observed. Morgan remained up at Sherrald's Ford, where he expected the British to appear, but also had hundreds of musket-wielding North Carolina militiamen led by General Davidson—"an active, zealous, and influential officer," Henry Lee concluded—guarding other nearby fords on the flooded river as he waited to see what the enemy would do.[176]

Once Greene received word from Morgan that the British had rapidly advanced from Winnsborough into North Carolina, the Rhode Islander decided that the time had come to unite his army's two distant wings. "I know they intend to bring me to an action," Morgan warned Greene in a January 25 dispatch, which he intend to avoid.[177] Two days later, Greene organized his troops at Hicks Creek into two brigades—one consisted of the Maryland Continentals under Colonel Otho Williams, "an accomplished gentlemen and experienced soldier," and the other was made up of Virginia troops led by Brigadier General Isaac Huger, a wealthy planter, Cherokee War (1760) veteran, and native South Carolinian. Soon afterward, Greene left the Pee Dee River camps and rode west to meet Morgan on the Catawba "with all imaginable haste," escorted by only three Continental dragoons across Tory-infested country. He left Huger in command at Hicks Creek and ordered him to march all the troops north along the east side of the Pee Dee (which is called the Yadkin in North Carolina) to Salisbury, where they could support Morgan.[178]

Greene reached Morgan's defensive post at Sherrald's Ford on January 30, where the wide river was still flooded. To Colonel William Campbell of western Virginia, the victorious commander at Kings Mountain in October, he requested "a thousand good militia from over the mountain" for one month's service, "to push the enemy," which would "give the world another proof of the bravery of the mountain militia." Greene also implored the militia officers of the Salisbury District to muster their companies "without loss of time" to oppose the redcoats. He also pressed General Huger to speed his movement to Salisbury. Greene wanted to "avoid an action" with the redcoats, who appeared determined to cross the Catawba and then race to Salisbury. "I beg you to hasten your march towards Salisbury as fast as possible." Concluding his letter, he advised Huger:

> *It is necessary we should take every possible precaution to guard against a misfortune. But I am not without hopes of ruining Lord Cornwallis if he persists in his mad scheme of pushing through the country and it is my earnest desire to form a junction* [of the army] *as soon as possible for this purpose.*

With this plan in mind, he also asked Huger to have Colonel Lee and his Legion join Morgan immediately with his Legion.[179]

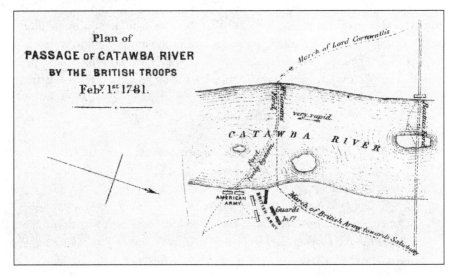

Nineteenth-century map of the Battle of Cowan's Ford. *From Hamilton,* The Grenadier Guards, *1874.*

Greene met with the senior Patriot officers on January 31 on the banks of the Catawba, including Morgan, Davidson, and Colonel Washington. Greene wanted Morgan and Davidson to hold the fords as long as possible and then fall back to Salisbury, but with few area militiamen coming into camp, Davidson's force was hopelessly small. "The people have been so harassed for eight months past," Greene reported to Congress, "and their domestic matters are in such distress that they will not leave home" but for a short time and were "of no use." Likewise, Greene reported to a local Carolina officer that although Davidson "has called out again and again for the people to turn out and defend their country," their "backwardness is unaccountable." Morgan's force at Sherrald's Ford was also too "inferior" to battle Cornwallis and lacked "provision and forage." Greene said "that we cannot hope for anything but a defeat" given the enemy's superior numbers and supplies.[180]

The Rhode Islander was right about the redcoats' intentions. With his army now "lightened" of its baggage, Cornwallis pressed his column forward at the Catawba. He ordered an infantry detachment to feint an attack at Beattie's Ford on the last day of January. Meanwhile, he led the rest of the army overnight to the actual intended crossing point at Cowan's Ford, four miles to the south, which was defended by General Davidson and 250 anxious North Carolina militia, some bearing long rifles, with about 50 dragoons. Here on February 1, 1,200 British troops supported by artillery boldly splashed across the cold river in an early morning fog and rain with "cool and determined bravery," Cornwallis stated. The Carolina militiamen initially put up a fight, even though they had been surprised by the British assault, but after Davidson was killed in the struggle, the rebels hastily retreated. A Carolina militiaman at the ford recorded:

> *We attempted to dispute the passage of the river with the enemy, but being protected by their cannon which were placed on a high hill opposite to us they succeeded in driving us from the ford and made good the crossing: we fought them as well as we could—we retreated and formed again on a hill about a half-mile from the ford where we made a stand—here Davidson was killed and many of the men: owing to a heavy rain that wetted our rifles we were unable to make a good defense and were driven from the field.*

Once hundreds of redcoats appeared on the east side of the Catawba, Morgan was forced to order all his troops to retreat to Salisbury and beyond to nearby Trading Ford on the Yadkin River, "very much swollen by the late rains," east of the town.[181] "The fall of Genl Davidson has left that people without an head in whom they have confidence as an officer," wrote North Carolina Patriot William Sharpe. "From my particular knowledge of that part of the country I can venture to say that in the fall of that officer we have lost more than 500 men in the common defence."[182]

The American forces now no longer had a major natural barrier to protect them from the oncoming British foe, which moved east with great speed. Protecting his army and its resources was Greene's paramount concern. With much of his militia scattered and the enemy in pursuit, he had some difficult decisions to take over the next few days.

Chapter 9

"Judiciously Designed and Vigorously Executed"

The Race to the Dan

Disciplined in the school of hard campaigning
Let the young Roman study how to bear
Rigorous difficulties without complaining
And camp with danger in the open air
—*Horace,* Odes, *"Dulce et Decorum Est, pro Patria Mori," 23 BC*

As Greene feared, Cornwallis was not slow to chase the retreating rebels once the Catawba fords were passed. Tarleton's dragoons pursued the American forces "in a violent rain" and successfully attacked and dispersed some four hundred of the militia with his dragoons at Tarrance's Tavern, ten miles east of Beattie's Ford on the Salisbury road. An Orange County militiaman later recalled that "shortly after that battle [of Cowan's Ford], the British dragoons charged the Americans at Torrence's Tavern several times—and at the time of the second charge, [he] was taken prisoner." A Chatham County man also recalled the scene, in which "they were pursued by a large number of British Light Horse and were overtaken and that they had to seek safety by flight into the woods[;] that some were killed and that he himself escaped." Cornwallis reported to Lord Germain that "this stroke, with our passage of the ford, so effectively dispirited the militia, that we met with no further opposition on our march to the Yadkin." The rest of Cornwallis's men followed Tarleton toward the Yadkin River, which they intended to cross at Trading Ford, burning several Patriot plantation houses along the route.[183]

Above: The site of Tarrant's Tavern was the scene of Tarleton's furious attack on militiamen after the battle at Cowan's Ford. *Author image.*

Opposite: The North Carolina Piedmont, from Salisbury to Hillsborough, also showing Guilford Courthouse. *Library of Congress.*

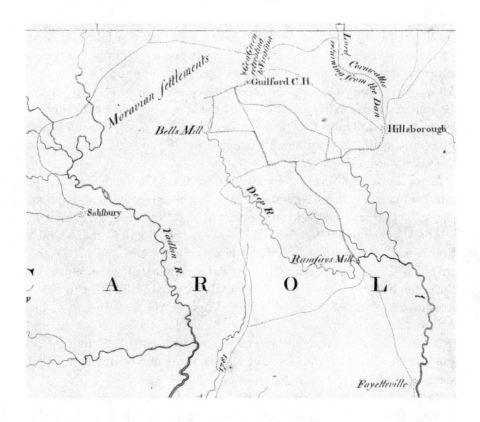

Greene also reported on the British pushing over the Catawba, threatening the rebels as they withdrew. "We made the best disposition we could to stop [the British] when the river should fall," Greene wrote, "but the fords were so numerous, and our force so small that we could not effect it." Greene's main force retired to Salisbury along the muddy road "in a hurry…in a cold dark night," according to a Rockingham County militiaman, and on February 2, they left that town for Trading Ford to the east. There the army crossed the Yadkin by boats the next day, while continuous rains made its waters rise rapidly.[184]

Cornwallis was less than a day's march behind the retreating rebels. His troops reached Salisbury on February 3, and the van of their column got to Trading Ford later that day. By then, most of the Americans had crossed the flooded river in boats and canoes, securing the far bank of the river. A Virginian wrote that "such was the ardor of pursuit that when we crossed to the north side of the Yadkin, the British were in full view on the south side of that stream." The British Guards and the von Bose Hessians, arriving at the ford in the lead of Cornwallis's column, briefly clashed with some rebel dragoons there, killed a few, and fired across the river, but to little effect. The von Bose men only "captured some prisoners and over 20 wagons laden with unimportant things." A Carolina militia quartermaster noted that that he was "able to get the military stores safely over the river, but was surprised by the British advance guard. There I lost my clothes & all my papers including my appointment in the Continental Army & that in the militia by General Davidson." It had been a close call.[185]

At Salisbury, the British rested on February 4, but Greene had his troops continue their march to Guilford Courthouse, a crossroads hamlet about sixty miles northeast on the main highway. Most of his men arrived there on February 7, including Huger's footsore soldiers from South Carolina whom Greene had redirected there. "Light-Horse Harry" Lee and his Legion arrived two days later. With his army now reunited, Greene entreated Governor Nash to muster more militia and asked von Steuben to hurry forward new Continental recruits from Virginia. "O that we had in the field, as Henry the Fifth said, some few of the many thousand that are idle at home," Greene lamented, misquoting Shakespeare from memory.[186] At Guilford Courthouse, Greene found that his ranks numbered about 2,000 soldiers, of which 1,426 were Continentals.[187]

Rather than pursue Greene directly from the deep, roiling waters at Trading Ford, Cornwallis and his redcoats and Hessians headed for the shallower upper Yadkin River fords. "I am much distressed by the rivers and creeks being swelled," he complained.[188] His troops crossed the chilly Yadkin River at Shallow Ford on February 9 and then advanced east to the Moravian towns, several settlements of German-speaking pietists who had moved to the Piedmont region from Pennsylvania in the early 1750s. Part of a dissenting pacifist Christian denomination originating in central Europe in the fourteenth century, by 1775 these prosperous farm families with "well-cultivated and fruitful plantations" had founded the towns of Bethania, Bethabara, and Salem, in modern Forsyth County. The British marched to these villages and helped themselves to food and supplies on February 9 and 10, plundering farms along their way.[189] One woman whose farm was along their route near Salem reported losing all she had:

> *The British Army passed by her house coming from the Shallow Ford on the Yadkin River* [to Salem] *& robbed her of all her corn, & small grain, meat and everything almost that her & family had to live on, even her ducks & chickens*[;] *some of them asked her if she had a husband* [and] *she said*

Reconstructed buildings at Bethabara, a Moravian town through which the British marched following Greene's retreating army. *Author image.*

Shallow Ford on the Yadkin River, where the British army crossed on their march to Salem. *Author image.*

Salem was a small, prosperous Moravian town through which the British army marched while chasing Greene's troops in February 1781. *Author image.*

yes: where is he they asked, she told them he was gone with a wagon to haul a load of ammunition to the American Army [and] *to shoot you red coats that have robbed me & my living.*[190]

At Salem, Cornwallis could see that from this favorable position about twenty-five miles west of Greene, the swift-moving British could march to attack the American army on the move if the rebels went north from Guilford to the upper crossings of the Dan River. The British general, of course, recognized that Greene and Morgan were likely to put yet another river between him and the American army, and the next major watercourse north/northeast of the rebels was the Dan. From the Moravian town, Cornwallis was almost as close to Dix's Ferry, a major crossing on the Dan River, as was Greene at Guilford Courthouse, a dangerous predicament for the harried rebels if indeed they planned to cross there. Additionally, the British commander could also trap "the American general on the lower Dan, which the great fall of rain rendered impassable without the assistance of boats, which [Cornwallis] supposed unattainable," recalled Colonel Lee.[191]

With the enemy so close, Greene and his senior officers had to decide the army's next move. Their critical situation was unfavorable for facing the British in a pitched battle. The militia refused to turn out, Cornwallis was just over a day's march to the west, and Greene's army was worn out. "It would be inevitable ruin to the army and no less ruinous to the American cause to hazard a general action," Greene advised Governor Nash. At a council of war Greene called, attended by Williams, Huger, and Morgan, the officers all agreed that the American army should march for the Dan River, cross it, and halt in Virginia. North Carolina, at least for a time, would be abandoned. "Nothing can be more painful than this measure," he despaired, "but a defeat is certain if we come to action" on the field of battle. Likewise, Greene predicted that "if I should risk a general action in our present situation, we stand ten chances to one of getting defeated, and if defeated all the southern states must fall." He had to protect his army, the symbol of the Patriot cause in the South. Moreover, Greene understood that a retreat would draw the already overstretched enemy even farther from its distant source of supplies at Charleston.[192]

But getting to Virginia safely with a fast-moving enemy to the rear was a dangerous maneuver. "Heavy rains, deep creeks, bad roads, poor horses and broken harness, as well as delays for want of provisions," in General Greene's evocative words, would also slow his army. Moreover, it took hours to cross an army over a wide river, during which time the enemy could catch the Americans in a vulnerable situation while ferrying the soldiers and guns and destroy them.[193]

With these fears in mind, Greene decided to split his army in two again. In order to slow the British pursuit, he established a light corps that would follow his army to prevent Cornwallis from attacking the main force and its slower wagons and artillery. This 700-man detachment consisted of Washington's dragoons, Lee's Legion, 60 Virginia mounted riflemen, and 280 Continental veterans of the Maryland, Delaware, and Virginia lines, commanded by Lieutenant Colonel John Eager Howard of Maryland. On February 10, Daniel Morgan had reluctantly left the army due to poor health, so Greene appointed Colonel Williams to lead this wing (and not General Huger, who outranked Williams but was "not known for individual initiative"). The rest of the army, including the guns and wagons, would be under Greene's direct command.[194]

Greene's intention was to reach safety north of the Dan River just across the Virginia border and ferry the troops by flatboats. Without watercraft of their own, the British would be unable to chase them across the river. Greene and his staff knew that the army could use three crossings: Dix's Ferry, a few miles below today's Danville; Irwin's Ferry, twenty miles downstream; and Boyd's Ferry, four miles farther down the river, at what is now South Boston. Greene had sent messages ahead to Colonel Carrington and other resourceful staff officers to collect all available boats on the river at Irwin's and Boyd's Ferries, where he planned to cross with his main army.

But Greene also had a trick to play on "the old fox," as some of the harried rebels dubbed Lord Cornwallis. Marching behind Greene's main body, Williams would start the light troops toward Dix's Ferry to dupe Cornwallis into chasing him rather than Greene, who instead would march to the downstream crossings; at some point, however, the light troops would have to march quickly to their right toward the lower Virginia fords, join Greene, and avoid the redcoats hanging on their rear while doing so. The unwary British did not know of Carrington's efforts to collect boats at the lower crossings, so they assumed that Greene, in advance of Williams's rear guard, would cross at the upper fords and ferry sites. They took the bait.[195]

Greene began to march his troops northeast toward Irwin's and Boyd's Ferries by February 10, while Colonel Williams moved with the light force to the northwest to locate the redcoats, slow their pursuit, and then fall back toward Dix's Ferry. Colonel Lee described their objective: "[T]he greater the distance between the main body and the light troops, the surer would be Greene's retreat." Williams placed Lee's dragoons in the rear, where they remained for most of what became known as "the Race to the Dan," which included numerous skirmishes between Williams's command and the van of Cornwallis's column, primarily Tarleton's cavalry, although no battles took place. Lee reported that once Cornwallis found his "corps of horse and foot close in front," the wary redcoats slowed down. Greene ordered Williams to be prudent as he delayed the enemy: "[Y]ou have the flower of the army, don't expose the men too much."[196]

The British troops now followed "with great rapidity" on the heels of the gritty light corps, pressing them from Hart's Old Stores near the Haw River and out of their cold camps at Chambers Mill on the upper reaches of Hogan's Creek. The lead ranks of the British column could often be seen from the rear of Williams's hard-pressed command during the march. The weary Americans walked almost without rest, often eating just one meal per day of bacon and ground corn. "On the road," Colonel

Dix's Ferry was a frequently used crossing site of the Dan River in Virginia, where Cornwallis expected Greene to bring his army. *Author image.*

Tarleton later recalled, "many skirmishes took place between the British and the American light troops, without great loss to either party, or any impediment to the progress of the main body."[197] A Botetourt County rifleman remembered the harrowing march vividly. The Virginians "were employed night and day on the lines throwing every difficulty in their power in the way of the advancing enemy. They were without tents and frequently without provisions and by privation of rest and sleep and every necessary comfort & excessive fatigue which brought on sickness and death in this inclement season of the year."[198]

While Williams scuffled with Cornwallis's aggressive cavalry and foot soldiers, Greene steadily pushed his column toward the Dan by way of High Rock Ford on the Haw River (in today's Rockingham County). "We marched for the most part both day and night," an American soldier recorded, "we had not scarce time to cook our victuals."[199] Greene noted that the march "was the most painful imaginable" and that hundreds of men were "tracking the ground with their bloody feet." Despite numerous letters from Greene to state leaders, the North Carolina militia all but abandoned him. Fearing for his supplies, the Yankee general ordered most of the army's stores at Hillsborough moved into Virginia to Prince Edward Court House and other magazines. Along the route, he received an alarming message from Williams on the wet night of the thirteenth/fourteenth—the enemy's main body was now only ten miles behind the light corps and closing fast. In fact, on the evening of February 14, Cornwallis, in an effort to make one final strenuous attempt to catch Greene, ordered his soldiers to leave their packs behind, and officers would only carry their arms and canteens. Rest was now out of the question. Williams could now no longer move toward Dix's Ferry, as by doing so he might expose the main column's rear to the harassing British cavalry. "Rely on it dear sir," Williams wrote anxiously, "it is possible for you to be overtaken before you reach the Dan....I shall use every precaution but cannot help being uneasy." And well he should have been, for as Colonel Lee later recalled, "more than once were the Legion of Lee and the van of [the British] within musket shot."[200]

On the morning of February 14, Greene ordered Williams to quit the road to Dix's Ferry and follow the main army on the road to Irwin's Ferry. Although at one point Williams thought his beleaguered column might ultimately have to be sacrificed on the south bank of the river to save the rest of the army, fortune smiled on American arms that day, as by 5:30 p.m. Greene's troops, guns, and few wagons were rowed across the Dan

The site of Boyd's Ferry on the Dan River, where part of Greene's army crossed in boats to avoid Cornwallis's pursuit in mid-February 1781. *Author image.*

River, crossing at both Boyd's and Irwin's Ferries. Having marched forty miles that day, Williams's fatigued troops arrived at Boyd's late that night and met by the anxious general. The light troops crossed without event.

The British did not appear on the south bank of the river until hours later, unable to cross for lack of boats. The ragged force of rebels "was safe over the river…laughing at the enemy who are on the opposite bank," wrote Greene's aide Major Burnet. Colonel Williams deemed the march one of Greene's "most masterly and fortunate maneuvers," and "the propriety of the retreat…has not been exceeded by any military maneuver practiced this war." Colonel Lee, whose troopers were the last to cross the Dan, summarized the "race" decades later in a tone that still showed his sense of relief. "Thus ended, on the night of the 14th of February, this long, arduous, and eventful retreat."[201]

Even Tarleton complimented Greene for his successful escape: "[O]wing to an excellent disposition, which was attended with some fortunate contingencies, General Greene passed the whole army over the river Dan on the 14th… without their receiving any materiel detriment from the King's troops. Every measure of the Americans, during their march from the Catawba to Virginia, was judiciously designed and vigorously executed."[202]

Perhaps the foremost modern historian of Nathanael Greene, Dennis M. Conrad, best summarized Greene's maneuvers in January and February 1781:

> *This retreat was a stunning achievement, more impressive because Greene's army lost virtually no men to desertion and was able to save his meager cache of supplies, even though the army's transport service was barely functioning. Moreover, the action highlights key elements of Greene's style of generalship: his knowledge of the southern terrain, his ability to make and revise plans quickly, his foresight, and probably most important his knowledge of his senior subordinates, which allowed him to assign to them tasks for which they were well suited.*[203]

All of these strengths would be put to the test over the following four weeks.

Chapter 10

"PILLAGING, PLUNDERING AND GETTING PROVISIONS"

Maneuvers in the Piedmont

In Squadrons came like fire and thunder
Men's hearts and heads both to pierce and plunder
Their errand was (when it was understood)
To bathe men's bosoms in a scarlet blood
—Zachary Boyd, 1640

When Lord Cornwallis arrived at Boyd's Ferry on the southern bank of the swirling, impassable Dan River on February 15, he was surely tired and frustrated. The target of his army's late exertions—fewer than two thousand hungry, exhausted rebels led by a former Rhode Island forge master—had escaped his pursuing veterans and were now inaccessible to attack from British arms. His Lordship and his senior officers were infuriated, having spent so much effort trying to bring the Americans to bay.[204]

The chase had come close to capturing or destroying the primary Patriot military force in the South, which would have annihilated the symbol of the cause of independence south of the Potomac River. Additionally, both Carolinas would have become British territory, with Virginia likely to fall next. Now that the wily Greene had eluded him, Cornwallis was forced to take stock of his precarious situation. The British were far from Charleston, from which they could be resupplied only with great difficulty, and no more reinforcements were expected soon. His army was tired, worn out, and needed to refit. Cornwallis was also out of touch with his superior, General Clinton in New York.

New York City and harbor in the 1780s, where Clinton made his headquarters. *Library of Congress.*

Several weeks later, Cornwallis would write a long letter to Germain in London with an account of this difficult campaign. Tarleton's defeat at Cowpens was a bitter pill to swallow, but "this event did not deter me from prosecuting the original plan" of invading North Carolina, he told the secretary. Indeed, Cornwallis's army moved with "great exertions." He had been joined by Leslie's reinforcements at Winnsborough in January, he told Germain, and tried to catch Morgan and liberate the redcoat prisoners of Cowpens. Rain-swollen creeks, excessive baggage, and Morgan's "celerity," however, prevented the British from overtaking him.[205]

Cornwallis reported to London with some pride that his army had turned into a light corps at Ramsour's Mill by burning baggage and all but the most necessary wagons, a decision his soldiers met with "chearfull acquiescence." He noted too that he forced the rebels back from the fords of the Catawba and pressed the enemy all the way to the Yadkin River "through one of the most rebellious tracts in America." But he was too late, he confessed to Germain, as the rebels had all the boats and the river continued to rise.[206]

At this point, the British general explained to Germain, he recognized that he had had to catch Greene's army as soon as possible, as the North

116

Carolina militia was not yet collected and Virginia had yet to support the rebel troops. Cornwallis concluded that Greene

> *would do everything in his power to avoid an action on the south side of the Dan; and, it being my interest to force him to fight, I made great expedition and got between him and the upper fords* [of the Dan], *and being assured that the lower fords are seldom practicable in winter and that he could not collect many flats* [boats] *at any of the ferrys, I was in great hopes that he would not escape me without receiving a blow.*

But despite "the patience and alacrity of the officers and soldiers under every species of hardship and fatigue," he had to admit to Germain that "all our exertions [were in] vain."[207]

Still, the British commander could find some advantages in his situation on the south bank of the Dan River. Greene and his worn-out army had been pushed out of North Carolina, which might now be open to a restoration of British rule. Moreover, few militiamen in the state turned out to bolster Greene's ranks as the Americans raced for the Dan, and Virginia seemed to provide little help to the rebel army. Although Cornwallis did not share the optimism of British leaders regarding the amount of support he could expect from southern Loyalists, his army controlled much of the state. It was now time to call forth the friends of the king to help restore royal authority and crush the rebellion.

Camped on the banks of the Dan, Cornwallis judged his own fatigued regiments "ill suited" to advance into the Old Dominion. With "North Carolina being in the utmost confusion," he decided to give his fatigued soldiers a day's rest and then "by easy marches" encamp at Hillsborough in Orange County, fifty miles to the south. The British column set out on February 16. Along the way, the redcoats encamped at Red House Church, a Presbyterian frame building built in the 1750s, about twenty-three miles southwest of Boyd's Ferry. Tradition holds that as they left the site, the British burned the church and the home of the recently deceased minister, Hugh McAden, whose fresh grave they vandalized.[208] The redcoats ravaged the countryside along their way, such as the property owned by James Irwin (also given as Irvine) and his family in Halifax County, who owned the ferry of their name and farmland just south of the Dan River. He "found that the British had reached the ferry...kept [owned] by himself & his brothers & had destroyed their farm, burnt their fences, destroyed their crop, killed their stock and at that point had turned back into North Carolina."[209]

Site of the eighteenth-century Red House Church, where British troops rested on their march to Hillsborough in February 1781. *Author image.*

On the twentieth, the plundering redcoats reached Hillsborough, where the men mended their ragged clothes and repaired battered shoes.[210] On the next day, Cornwallis "erected the King's standard," a centuries-old tradition of announcing to the populace that all able-bodied men loyal to the sovereign should arm themselves and come forward to fight on the Crown's behalf. "The royal flag was hoisted with a salute of 21 guns," noted a Hessian soldier, but the general got little support from the Loyalists, despite the unusual fanfare. Tarleton noted that many nearby inhabitants "rode into the British camp, to talk over the proclamation, inquire the news of the day, and take a view of the King's troops." But few of them joined the ranks.[211]

Cornwallis also sought to establish communications with British-held Wilmington on the lower Cape Fear River in order to be resupplied by way of Cross Creek, about one hundred miles south of his position. By this time, the soldiers desperately needed shoes, "cavalry appointments" were worn out, and the army had few wagons. An officer with Greene's army reported that "protecting the friends of government, procuring shoes for his Army which at present they are much in want of; and collecting provisions seems to actuate his Lordship's conduct in some measure." Cornwallis also wrote to Lieutenant Colonel Nesbit Balfour, officer in charge at Charleston, asking for any available reinforcements. Ominously, he also reported that Greene was rumored to be receiving large numbers of militia in his Virginia camps.[212] Cornwallis's intelligence was correct: Greene's army was indeed growing, along with American fortunes.

Wasting no time after successfully bringing his depleted army safely into Virginia, Greene dispatched a flurry of letters over the next several days from Irwin's Ferry and his headquarters at Halifax Court House on the Bannister River, several miles to the north of Boyd's Ferry, to bring in supplies and more soldiers. He had only two hundred militia and feared a British attack once the Dan River receded to become passable. He encouraged officers to raise mounted infantry for the campaign, and from Governor Jefferson he asked for dragoons, more militia led by experienced officers, supplies, and equipment, "or the country is inevitably lost." From the North Carolina legislature, he requested hundreds of militiamen, "a good body of riflemen," and "superior cavalry." Having learned his lesson well over the past two weeks, he advised that "the troops that take the field [should] be as lightly equipped as possible, for Lord Cornwallis moves with great rapidity." He asked for six hundred muskets and cartridge boxes from von Steuben at Chesterfield Court House in Virginia and worried that Cornwallis would chase him farther north or that the British would head east to Halifax, North Carolina, where supplies were more plentiful. The Americans would soon be "ruined without reinforcements." Now that the British were no longer chasing his command, Greene thought that the North Carolina militia would begin to arrive in camp, joined by more from Virginia. "I have some expectation of collecting a force sufficient in this country to enable me to act offensively," he wrote optimistically, "and in turn race Lord Cornwallis as he has done me."[213]

By February 18, Greene reported that the militia in nearby Virginia counties south of the James River were gathering for about six weeks of service with him, and he planned to have more North Carolina militia under General Caswell join him if possible. He heard that hundreds of mounted riflemen from mountainous western Virginia were riding to join him, led by Colonels William Preston and William Campbell. He also ordered Brigadier General Andrew Pickens of South Carolina, now in temporary command of all of the western militia operating around Guilford Courthouse, to use his force of several hundred men to "harass the enemy's rear," although many of Pickens's troops were deserting daily.[214]

Greene soon realized that he had to cross the Dan River back into North Carolina. He could not let Cornwallis "roam at large," showing Carolinians that the British had retaken the war-ravaged state. That could lead to Tories turning out to reinforce the redcoats and violence against Patriots. Moreover, as one militiaman later wrote, the Americans had to prevent the British from "pillaging, plundering and getting provisions." Greene "instantly determined as the most effectual measure to prevent it to advance into the state" without waiting for additional reinforcements from Virginia, he wrote to Governor Jefferson. "It was necessary to convince the Carolinians that they were not conquered."[215]

Andrew Pickens, a South Carolina militia general who fought at the Battle of Cowpens, also commanded part of Greene's militia before the battle at Guilford Courthouse. *Library of Congress.*

Greene indeed began to "act offensively" as more militia companies joined him. As early as February 19, Greene planned to move south and attack the enemy's rear as the redcoats marched toward Hillsborough. Lee's Legion and some Maryland troops, strengthened by a detachment of Guilford County militia, crossed the Dan to scout the enemy's position that day, soon followed by Williams with the light infantry. Within days, they were close enough to the enemy's camps to capture thirsty redcoats in search of whiskey beyond their sentries at night.[216]

Greene's main army left its camp near Halifax Court House, crossed the Dan on February 22 at Boyd's Ferry, and set out toward Hillsborough. His force was too small for an attack, such that "our movements must be cautious which will put it out of our power to effect anything capital," partly due to the "uncertainty of the militia," which Greene deemed a poor "barrier in the field" against British designs.[217]

General Pickens's militia joined Lee's cavalry on February 23 close to Hillsborough. They "kept ranging about through the county with a view of keeping the British from furnishing their regular army with provisions," recalled a Surrey County veteran.[218] That same day, they successfully attacked a small British post at Hart's Mill, two miles from the town. Greene, however, kept the main army at a respectful distance, marching southwest from Boyd's Ferry along the east side of Country Line Creek

"Pyle's Massacre" likely occurred along this road trace near Hillsborough in 1781. *Mark Bradley.*

angling toward High Rock Ford on the Haw River. The troops were "exceedingly distressed for want of provisions," and many soldiers had not eaten in "three or four days."[219]

Although few Loyalists came forth to join Cornwallis's army during the campaign, one Tory formation in the field was that of an English-trained doctor, Colonel John Pyle, a longtime supporter of the Crown. He had raised a mounted militia force of several hundred men in the district between the Haw and Deep Rivers, in Guilford and Chatham Counties, both being prominent for disaffection from the Patriot cause. Pyle was scouting west of Hillsborough for rebel militia and Greene's troops at the same time that Lee and Pickens were operating in the area. Pyle was also trying to link up with Tarleton, whose Legion was close by but whom Pyle could not locate.[220]

For two days, Pickens and Lee warily followed Tarleton west of the Haw River, trying to "alarm the enemy by night and harass them by day." On February 25, the Americans came upon Pyle's militia halted in column along a roadway near Holt's Plantation (also called "The Races") in what is now Alamance County. Pyle's horsemen mistook Lee's dragoons for Tarleton's Legion as they rode by, as both mounted units wore short green regimental coats and Tarleton was known to be in the neighborhood. Lee used this ruse to have his mounted column come along even with the unsuspecting Tories and then suddenly attacked with their swords. More than ninety Loyalists were "most inhumanly butchered," and more were wounded in what came to be known as "Pyle's Massacre." One of Pickens's men wrote that "a great slaughter was made of the Tories whilst they were crying out that they were friends of King George." Lee's dragoons hacked at the Tories so furiously that several of them bent their swords in the action. A Patriot militiaman recalled seeing six Tory prisoners in camp "hewed to pieces with broadswords" the evening after the battle, such was the animosity among Carolinians at the time. This slaughter quelled Loyalist support for Cornwallis in the Piedmont, and few, if any, friends of the king joined his army afterward.[221]

After this bloody defeat, Cornwallis ordered Tarleton back to Hillsborough, while Lee and Pickens—just reinforced by Colonel Preston's three hundred Botetourt County, Virginia militiamen—remained along the Haw River. With growing numbers, Greene pushed out his screening force of light infantry under Colonel Williams toward Hillsborough as the American army continued to move toward High Rock Ford, between Hillsborough and Guilford Courthouse. At the end of the month, Cornwallis shifted all his troops west toward Alamance Creek, a tributary of the Haw, still scarce on provisions, "plundering and distressing the country," "notwithstanding every

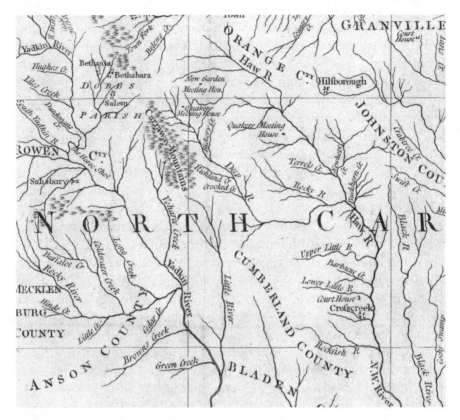

Central North Carolina, with the Moravian towns and New Garden Meeting House in upper left. *Library of Congress.*

order, every entreaty that Lord Cornwallis has given the army," notably to the women camp followers.[222]

Captain Graham of the Mecklenburg County militia remembered the next two weeks of the campaign as a "game of checkers," while General O'Hara of the Guards noted that "the two armies were never twenty miles asunder, they constantly avoiding a general action and we industriously seeking it. These operations obliged the two armies to make numberless moves, which it is impossible to detail." A North Carolinian in the ranks wrote that Greene "kept the Army in almost constant motion not suffering it to encamp on the same ground two nights in succession," and a Virginian recalled that "the movements of the army consisted of marching to and fro, sometimes hanging upon Cornwallis and at others flying from him." More recently, historians Jim Piecuch and John Beakes described the maneuvers as a period of "frequent encounters between the parties and screening forces of the two armies, as both Greene and Cornwallis sought to gain a position that would offer the best advantage in a major battle." All the while, Greene's force continued to suffer from many wants.[223]

Detachments of the two belligerents fought a number of small engagements in the Piedmont during this period. When British and American troops under Tarleton and Lee skirmished at Clapp's Mill south of Big Alamance Creek on March 4, the hard-pressed Americans had to retreat.[224] Two days later, at Weitzel's Mill on Reedy Fork Creek, a major British detachment clashed with Williams's light troops and militia, who were screening Greene's army but separated from the main body by the creek. After sharp fighting, the redcoats pushed across the creek and compelled Williams to withdraw, but the American forces fought well that day. A Virginia officer in the engagement remembered it as "a severe battle with Cornwallis's army at Whitesell's Mill on the Reedy Fork of the Haw River, where we lost a good many worthy men in killed and wounded, and there we lost the chief of the baggage belonging to our regiment." The result of this sharp engagement led General Greene to bring all of his troops north of the Haw River at High Rock Ford by March 10, which put him closer to the reinforcements he expected from Virginia and placed a water obstacle between his ranks and Cornwallis.[225]

Site of High Rock Ford on the Haw River. *Jeffrey P. Oves.*

Still, logistics continued to plague the American troops, as Greene reported to General Washington that "the want of supplies in this country, the superiority of the enemy and the mode in which the militia do duty, are alarming circumstances at this critical period."[226] A Virginia officer with the army wrote that "the army has been much in want of provision…their future prospects of supplies are by no means promising tho the soldiers bear all the vicissitudes of a military life without repining."[227]

The rebel army also needed reinforcements to have any chance of success against the enemy. By early March, many of the dispirited Carolina militia companies had gone home, claiming that their tours were over. Others deserted in droves when Greene had their horses taken away, since the mounts consumed too much local forage. Some of Pickens's militia were also angered that they had been poorly deployed (they claimed) by Williams at Weitzel's Mill and suffered high casualties as a result. A Virginia officer with the army reported the scene to Governor Jefferson:

> The riflemen complained that the burthen, and heat, of the day was entirely thrown upon them, and that they were to be made a sacrifice by the regular officers to screen their own troops. Full of this idea, the greater number left the light troops. Some rejoined their regiments with the main body and others thought it a plausible excuse for their return home.

One of the riflemen recalled that "a few days after[,] Col. Campbell offered to let his rifle men return home, many of whom had lost their horses and blankets, and were badly equipped, for a winter campaign, and nearly all of them accepted his kind offer." Pickens lost virtually his entire command; so many disgruntled militiamen left that Greene agreed with Pickens that the latter should march the Georgia and South Carolina men still in his ranks back home within days.[228]

While hundreds of militiamen abandoned Greene, Cornwallis too was left with a strategic problem. Supplies were hard to come by in the long picked-over area, and he was far from British stores and magazines in South Carolina and at Wilmington. Some of his senior lieutenants wanted him to chase Greene's retreating troops after the action at Weitzel's Mill, press their advantage, and position the army between the Americans and anticipated reinforcements marching from Virginia. Tarleton, always aggressive, in particular pleaded for an offensive:

An immediate movement of the King's Troops across High Rock Ford might, at this period, have produced various and decisive events. Such a maneuver might have intercepted the American stores and reinforcements, then approaching from Hillsborough and Virginia; might have interrupted the retreat of the American army, or force the Continentals to hazard an action without the assistance of their eighteen month men or militia… vigorous exertions for forty-eight hours would procure favorable opportunities of taking all the stores of the Americans, beating their army in detail, and securing the event of the campaign.

But with serious supply problems, more cautious officers recommended moving west to the Deep River, where provisions could be procured among Quaker settlements there (around today's Jamestown). Cornwallis adopted the latter suggestion, in effect leaving the rebels alone for the time being. This prudent move, he thought, would continue to secure the Loyalists in the region and allow him to "approach the communication of our shipping on the Cape Fear River, which I saw would soon become indispensably necessary to open on account of the sufferings of the army."[229]

Marching briskly on the Great Salisbury Road, the British reached the Deep River Friends (Quaker) Meeting House on March 13, by way of Guilford Courthouse, twelve miles to the northeast, shadowed by Colonel Williams's harassing light corps all the way. Neither the rebels nor redcoats knew that within forty-eight hours, the culminating battle of the wearisome campaign would be fought.[230]

Chapter 11

"An Engagement Now Became Inevitable"

The Armies Prepare for Battle

Cavalry! Troop after troop it spills
With strange insignia, strangely armed,
As snow in a spring thaw fills

The Valley roads. From the forests long
Bright bayonets issue, as brigades of foot
Debouch like ants, form up, and densely throng;

All heading north...

—*Adam Mickiewicz, "The Year 1812"*[231]

Greene continued to stay north of the protective Haw River after the action at Weitzel's Mill, varying the army's position around High Rock Ford and nearby Speedwell Ironworks on Troublesome Creek.[231] He "dissolved" Colonel Williams's light corps on March 9 and added these troops back to the main army. Williams would now serve as the army's adjutant general and commander of the Maryland Continentals. Lee and his mounted troops, along with Washington's Continental dragoons, now operated as "parties of observation," as close as was safe to the British, who by this time were en route to the forks of the Deep River. Lee and Washington were each bolstered by several hundred mounted riflemen, to allow them to "give the enemy all annoyance in [their] power."[232] The British movements were closely observed by the American army. "Lord Cornwallis, in taking his present Position, seems to have two objects in view," Major Charles Magill, a Virginia officer, reported to Thomas Jefferson: one, "cutting off supplies from Virginia, at least making them take a more circuitous route. The other to bring our Army to a general action, before any number of the militia can possibly join us."[233]

On March 10, Greene reported that he had several hundred halfhearted militia in camp at High Rock Ford, but so many were constantly arriving and then leaving once they became "tired out with difficulties" that he could make no firm estimate of the strength of his command. "I am vexed to my soul with the militia, they desert us by hundreds, nay by thousands."[234] The general sensed that he was expected by the people of the southern states to come to battle with the British but dared not risk it until reinforced. However, he soon expected more than one thousand short-term militia from eastern North Carolina, and once they appeared, he would advance toward the enemy.[235]

Starting late on March 10, Greene finally saw hundreds of long-awaited soldiers begin to march into his riverside camp. Brigadier General Robert Lawson's Virginia militia had arrived by the eleventh, with men from the Southside counties of Amelia, Cumberland, Powhatan, Mecklenburg, and Brunswick brigaded for the campaign. Greene organized a second brigade of Virginia militia, led by General Edward Stevens, with militia from the counties of Pittsylvania, Halifax, Lunenburg, Prince Edward, Augusta, and Rockbridge. These men were "tolerably well-armed, the greater part I believe their own private property." One Virginian wrote in praise of Stevens's men:

> *It must however be said to the honor of the middle & back counties, that upon the approach of Cornwallis, no time, not even the Year 75 ever exhibited a more hearty zeal in the common cause. Old men, who had long laid aside the Musket, even half Tories caught the Flame.*

Also on the tenth, a large body of North Carolina militia led by Generals John Butler and Thomas Eaton strengthened Greene's host as well, with about 1,200 men.[236]

No doubt Greene placed his hopes for success on his regulars. General Huger commanded the army's two Virginia battalions of Continentals, which had just been strengthened by several hundred new recruits enlisted for eighteen months, who "by the unexpected arrival of some cloathing from

Greene's army camped along Troublesome Creek before and after the Battle of Guilford Courthouse. *Author image.*

Philadelphia were at length equipped and sent in two detachments to General Greene" from Chesterfield Court House. The 1st Virginia Regiment's commander was a former Quaker, Colonel John Green, who had been an officer since 1775, and his troops were a combination of veterans and new recruits. The 2nd Virginia consisted almost entirely of the new levies, only a few with previous Continental service, disciplined by Baron von Steuben and commanded by Lieutenant Colonel Samuel Hawes.[237]

Colonel Williams still led the Marylanders, recently reorganized as the 1st and 2nd Maryland Regiments. The 1st Maryland, commanded by Somerset County native Colonel John Gunby, was one of the most experienced, reliable units in Continental service and had fought in many of the American army's major battles. The remnants of the Delaware Regiment, which took heavy losses at Camden, was also included in the ranks. Lieutenant Colonel Benjamin Ford, a veteran officer from St. Mary's County, led the inexperienced 2nd Maryland, which had been raised the previous summer from across the state, had few veterans in its ranks, and had only joined Greene a few days before the battle. Each of the two commands numbered about four hundred soldiers tolerably armed and equipped. Greene's force also consisted of three light infantry companies from Virginia and Maryland; a small North Carolina Continental company; two companies of militia dragoons; and two sections of Continental Artillery, each with two six-pounder guns (two of which had been captured at Cowpens). In total, the southern American army had just over four thousand men present with Greene along the Haw River, which they left on March 12 for Guilford Courthouse.[238]

MAJOR GENERAL BARON STEUBEN.

Major General Baron von Steuben served as Greene's chief logistician in Virginia, supporting the Southern Campaign. *Library of Congress.*

Many historians have concluded that when Greene moved his army to Guilford Courthouse, he intended to take up a defensive position there and await an inevitable British assault. These writers almost invariably state that when Greene and the army camped there in early February, he decided then that the ground around the courthouse would make an excellent position to receive an attack and thus maneuvered his command to a predetermined deployment on advantageous hills and ridges until Cornwallis advanced against the rebel lines.

Contrary to this common narrative, the American commander was thinking offensively before the battle. In early February, he wrote to General Huger that "I wish to be prepared, either for attacking or for receiving one." Corresponding to Governor Jefferson on March 10, Greene noted that he hoped "to encumber the enemy with a number of wounded men," perhaps by an attack. Also, in a March 10 letter, Major Magill wrote to Jefferson that "the troops at present indulge the most pleasing expectations, and anticipate the happiness they hope to enjoy by making the British shortly retreat before them with precipitation," which implies an active American advance. On the thirteenth, one of the Virginia militia officers wrote home that the army marched the previous day "to look for Cornwallis" and also reported on the fourteenth that the American army was "marching to attack Cornwallis." Greene's letter to Henry Lee the day before the battle also reveals that he intended to press forward from the courthouse crossroads toward the British

Site of the original Guilford County Courthouse, near which Greene posted his Continentals along the Old Salisbury Road. *Author image.*

where they rested at Deep River, twelve miles to the south. Cornwallis too noted that on the same afternoon that he received intelligence that Greene, now reinforced, "was marching to attack the British troops." The colonel of the Guilford County militia, James Martin, wrote that Greene "resolved to move towards the British to give them battle," and only after "hearing that the British were moving towards him" did he adopt a defensive position. The clearest indication of Greene's plans was his post-battle report to Congress, in which he stated that with his army enlarged by Continentals and militia on the tenth, "I took the resolution of attacking the enemy without loss of time." Now with four thousand soldiers, the Southern Department commander could finally risk a battle with the enemy. Although not expecting Cornwallis to move the next day, Greene wrote on the fourteenth to Lee that "if they [the British] should [move] it will be to attack us. I only dread two things, a heavy rain and a night attack," alluding to the superiority in the use of the bayonet by British troops, which rain and darkness would enhance. He closed with a prudent warning to Lee: "[D]on't get surprised, nor let us be so."[239]

An original pattern 1768 bayonet, commonly used by British troops during the Revolutionary War. *Private collection.*

Greene now had his reinforced army just a dozen miles from the enemy, with no major river in between them and with a proper road linking their positions. Given the danger of Tarleton's fearsome dragoons and the British light troops, the Continental commander had to be watchful. To guard against surprise and watch the redcoats, Greene sent the cavalry of Lee and Washington—bolstered by riflemen and infantry—in front of his army late on March 14, with Lee to the left and Washington off to the right. Cautiously, he also ordered a militia detachment "with a parcel of the baggage wagons belonging to the Army north across [Reedy Fork] creek which lay about 2 miles off and they were directed after they crossed to take up the bridge and await further orders."[240]

The American soldiers cooked their rations on the night of the fourteenth and prepared to march closer to the British early the next day. Although Greene planned an offensive maneuver in the morning, that evening Greene and his staff—including Colonels Davie, Lewis, and Carrington—also considered that their army's position by the courthouse was well suited for defense. Having previously halted his troops at the hamlet in early February, Greene knew the terrain in the area; there were also numerous Guilford County natives in his militia ranks to advise him. The Great Salisbury Road, known locally as the New Garden Road since it ran by the New Garden Friends meetinghouse four miles south, was the only route of approach for the British to come at him and was hemmed in by thick, brushy woods on both sides. The forests would limit enemy artillery fire, disrupt neat, double lines of advancing redcoats, and restrict Tarleton's cavalry in their movements as well. Several wooded ridges would serve to give his own troops good defensive positions, if needed. "The greater part of this country is a wilderness," he reported, "with a few cleared fields interspersed here and there."[241] It must have been a restless night for Greene. Although one veteran of the battle recalled decades later that "General Greene rode from company to company making speeches to his men and exhorting them to stand by their country," little is known of the general's actions on the eve of battle.[242]

Lord Cornwallis, of course, had his own plans. Provisions had become difficult to obtain by the British camps in the Deep River area, which turned out to be "exhausted country." Consequently, Cornwallis tried to open communications with Cross Creek and Wilmington for resupply, which he deemed "indispensably necessary." Yet the combative general was not shrinking from a battle. "I was determined to fight the rebel army if it approached me," he wrote. Once Greene moved to his north at Guilford Courthouse, Cornwallis was "persuaded that [Greene] had resolved to hazard an engagement" and decided to "meet the enemy or attack them in their encampment." It was a plan similar to the one he adopted at Camden the previous summer. Tarleton too recorded that Cornwallis "had the alternative, either to commence his retreat, or prepare for a general action." But with Greene now so close, the choice was obvious. Overnight Cornwallis ordered the army's wounded, wagons, and baggage to be moved south under an escort of Hamilton's Loyalist regiment and twenty British Legion dragoons down the Deep River about twelve miles to Bell's Mill. The army was then set in motion north on the Salisbury Road at 4:00 a.m., without breakfast.[243]

In the rainy early morning hours of March 15, the watchful Colonel Lee began to suspect a British advance toward the courthouse. From an advanced post three miles in front of the rebel army on the New Garden Road, Lee sent a detachment of his dragoons farther ahead to spy on the enemy near the Deep River Quaker farms. They detected troops stirring and wagons moving in the darkness in the enemy camps. By 4:00 a.m., this intelligence reached Lee, who then informed Greene. Lee soon received orders from his commander to push his Legion, some riflemen, and a small detachment of Virginia Continentals forward toward the New Garden Meeting House for more information.[244]

Just as Lee sent his troopers down the road to find signs of the enemy, Tarleton's cavalry was in the van of the oncoming British column, headed for the courthouse. In a series of three "sharp" skirmishes on the New Garden Road beginning around sunrise, Lee's advance detachment and Tarleton's troops, including supporting infantry of the 23rd Regiment, bloodied each other over approximately two hours that morning. Lee and his command "behaved with the most undaunted bravery and maintained himself against the most formidable opposition," wrote a British soldier in the fighting. After these close-up engagements (one of which took place around the Quakers' meetinghouse), during which he was thrown from his horse, Lee saw the British main column approaching from Deep River and retired to

Site of the crossroads along New Garden Road where the forces of Lee and Tarleton clashed on the morning of March 15. *Author image.*

the American army's position, now certain that the entire enemy force was moving toward Greene's camps. Both Tarleton and Lee each claimed in their memoirs to have bested the enemy in the confrontations.[245]

Lee's timely dispatches to Greene in the early morning of March 15 not only alerted the general to the British advance but also led him to adopt a defensive posture for the contest he now knew was coming. Thus, while Lee fought Tarleton several miles to his front, Greene deployed his army by the courthouse for his first battle in the South.

Greene's battle plan was based on the lessons of the engagements of Camden and Cowpens, as well as the advice of General Morgan. Greene was well aware of Gates's deployment of his army at Camden the previous summer, where he placed his unreliable militia troops on his left flank, with no regulars immediately behind them for support. The result, as earlier described, was a rout. At Cowpens, however, Morgan recognized his militia's shortcomings and used it masterfully to his advantage. Placed in the front two lines with limited a role, the militia blunted Tarleton's attack, retired in good order, and helped win the day.

Greene also relied on Morgan's letter to him of February 20, after the victor of Cowpens had left the army due to poor health:

> *I suspect Lord Cornwallis will push you till you are obliged to fight him[,] on which much will depend. You'll have from what I see, a great number of militia—if they fight you'll beat Cornwallis[,] if not, he will beat you and perhaps cut your regulars to pieces, which will be losing all our hopes. I am informed among the militia will be a number of old soldiers. I think it would be advisable to select them from among the militia, and put them in the ranks of the regulars[;] select riflemen also, and fight them on the flanks under enterprising officers who are acquainted with that kind of fighting and put the remainder of the militia in the center with some picked troops to their rear with orders to shoot down the first man that runs[;] if anything will succeed a disposition of this kind will.*[246]

While Greene did not pull the veterans out of the militia ranks, he did take some of Morgan's suggestions and to a large extent based his army's deployment on the example of the Cowpens victory.

Site of the skirmish around the New Garden Meeting House on the morning of the battle. *Author image.*

Greene arranged his army in three lines, a defense in depth designed to blunt the British onslaught as it advanced along the New Garden Road, their likely route of approach. As Morgan had done in January, Greene established his front line with militia. On a low ridge perpendicular to the roadway several hundred yards west of the courthouse, he deployed Eaton's North Carolina brigade to the north (right) of the road. This brigade included militia from Warren, Franklin, Nash, Edgecombe, Halifax, Martin, and Northampton Counties, in the eastern part of the state. South of the road, Butler's militia companies from Caswell, Granville, Orange, Guilford, Rowan, Mecklenburg, Chatham, and Randolph Counties fell into line, men from central North Carolina. "We were stationed by General Greene behind a fence," wrote a militiaman in the first line, "that being a position which he thought most advantageous for raw troops who were unaccustomed to stand the shock of battle." Heeding Morgan's advice to "select riflemen…and fight them on the flanks," Greene situated experienced troops on both ends of this first line, including regulars. On his far left, he placed Campbell's sixty Virginia riflemen, a company of Virginia Continentals, and Lee's Legion, trying to rest after the morning's fighting. On the right of the Carolina militia, he posted Colonel Charles Lynch's Virginia riflemen form Bedford County, with some Virginia militia cavalry, a few dozen ill-equipped mounted North Carolinians, Washington's 3rd Continental Light Dragoons, and a steady Delaware Continental company under Captain Robert Kirkwood, a young officer with several years of combat experience behind him. Then, two Continental Artillery brass six-pounder cannons commanded by Captain Anthony Singleton were placed in the road at the top of the rise, supported by a company of about fifty North Carolina Continentals nearby.[247]

About three hundred yards behind (east of) the first line, Greene placed the Virginia militia, with Steven's brigade south of the road and Lawson's north of it. This second line was in heavily wooded land with thick brush on the forest floor, limiting visibility as well as the officers' command and control of the troops. Most of the ground here was relatively flat, but it dropped off in their rear. Here, Samuel Houston, a Rockbridge County volunteer, recalled that the militia's "brigade major came, ordering [us] to take trees as we pleased. The men run to choose their trees, but with difficulty, many crowding to one, and some far behind others. But we moved by order of our officers, and stood in suspense."[248]

On high ground about five hundred yards behind the Virginia militia, just west of the courthouse on the New Garden Road overlooking an overgrown, open field and a sluggish, winding stream called Hunting Creek, Greene

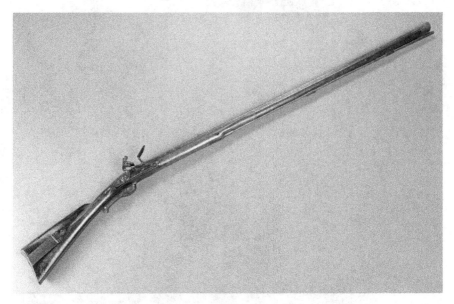

A 1760s flintlock long rifle, typical of those used by southern militiamen in the Guilford Courthouse campaign. *Scott Metzler image for the National Museum of the U.S. Army.*

placed his third line, consisting of his Continental infantry, all of which were north of the road. The 2nd Maryland, with its left flank on the road, extended northward. Immediately to its right was the veteran 1st Maryland. The third line continued north, with the 2nd Virginia in wooded ground and Colonel Green's more experienced 1st Virginia being on the army's far right flank. By placing the Continentals in the third line, Greene acted to preserve the core of his army—his regulars. Two guns of the Continental Artillery were sited near Green's regiment with a wide field of fire. The third line was just west of the Reedy Fork Road, which led northward from Guilford Courthouse to Speedwell Ironworks.[249]

Once in position, the troops loaded their muskets, checked their flints, finished eating their breakfasts, and sought advantageous firing positions. And then they waited for the British to come. "We were ordered to stand firm and do what we could," an Orange County militiaman on the first line wrote, and doubtless they listened nervously to the gunshots off to the west as "Light-Horse Harry" Lee and his nimble detachment skirmished with enemy forces uniformed in green and red.[250]

After the early morning fighting on the New Garden Road, Cornwallis continued his steady approach toward the courthouse in a light rain. He could get no accurate information on Greene's position or "a description of

American artillery posted on Greene's third line near the courthouse site at Guilford Courthouse National Military Park. *Author image.*

the ground." The long column crossed a rivulet called Horsepen Creek and then arrived at the small farm of the Hoskins family next to the road, with several cleared fields around it, notably to the right. There they saw, ahead in the wood line, armed Americans waiting on the other side of the overgrown land to their front.[251]

Cornwallis used the New Garden Road as an axis for the Crown force's deployment and advance, which was to be a head-on attack. To the left of the road, Lieutenant Colonel James Webster commanded the red-coated troops, with the 23rd Foot, consisting of 238 soldiers just north of the road, and next to them, the 33rd Foot, with 234 officers and men in the ranks. Behind these tough veterans of Bunker Hill, Long Island, Brandywine, Monmouth, Charleston, and Camden were the grenadiers and light infantry of the Guards—the elite companies of British regiments—along with the company of green-coated, rifle-wielding Hessian Jaegers. On the right (south) side of the road, General Leslie commanded the British soldiers. In his front line next to the road was the 2nd Battalion of the 71st Regiment, with 244 Highlanders in their lines.

To their right was the Regiment von Bose, with 321 Hessian soldiers in their dark blue regimental coats, led by Major Johan Christian Du Buy, a Seven Years' War veteran and soldier since age fourteen. Behind them in support were the two battalions of the elite Guards, more than 472 men drawn for American service from all three British Guards regiments and led by General O'Hara. The Royal Artillery guns commanded by First Lieutenant John McLeod took up a position on the road near the farm buildings. Tarleton's Legion, with a small troop of the 17th Light Dragoons attached, remained just to the rear of Cornwallis's front ranks, poised on the road to exploit any break in the rebel lines.[252]

With the tired, hungry British troops now pushed out in long lines to the left and right of the muddy road, bayonets fixed, the stage was set by just after 1:00 p.m. As Tarleton succinctly put it, "[A]n engagement now became inevitable."[253]

Chapter 12

"Dreadful Was the Havoc on Both Sides"

The Attack of the King's Army

The game's afoot!
Follow your spirit, and upon this charge
Cry, "God for Harry, England, and Saint George!"
—*William Shakespeare*, Henry V, *Act 3, Scene I*

The American army was in position by 11:00 a.m., poised for battle. Many of these waiting soldiers and militiamen had been marching across the Carolinas for months in winter weather, maneuvering to avoid the enemy, while others were newly raised troops with little military experience. Some had tasted bitter defeat at Camden or the excitement of victory at Kings Mountain and Cowpens. Now, with the British approaching Greene's defensive lines, all knew that the climactic battle would soon begin.

Like General Morgan before the Battle of Cowpens, Greene rode along the first line of anxious North Carolina militia at the fence to encourage them, asking them to "fire two volleys and then retire" to the second line. Then, likely before the redcoats appeared, Greene returned to the courthouse ridge. Soon afterward, Colonel Lee also gave a short oration to steel some of the militia companies, telling them that he had already beaten the British three times that morning on the New Garden Road and would do it again. "My brave boys," young Lee supposedly yelled from his saddle, "your lands, your lives and your country depend on your conduct today." He then rode off to his Legion's position on the army's left, "in a great rage for battle," noted an impressed militiaman, while another soldier recalled that Lee "told

Greene posted his North Carolina militia companies here at the first line, overlooking the Hoskins farm. *Author image.*

them it would be sufficient if they would stand to make only two fires: there then appeared to be blood on his sword" from the morning's combat on the New Garden Road.[254]

From the Carolinians' ranks at the tree line east of the Hoskins house, the British were at last spotted coming uphill on the New Garden Road, their red coats clearly visible through the leafless trees, as were their unfurled regimental colors. Once at the Hoskins farmstead, Cornwallis deployed his regiments, ready to attack across the open field, which had been recently plowed and was wet and muddy from the recent rains.

While the British troops were deploying at the bottom of the slope west of the rebel ranks, Cornwallis ordered his artillery to bombard Greene's center. Tarleton stated that "as the front of the British column approached the open ground facing the American position, the enemy's six-pounders opened from the road, and were immediately answered by the royal artillery." Firing three guns at the militia, "the British artillery cannonaded the enemy's center with considerable effect." The two rebel cannons under Captain Singleton answered effectively, and their fire killed Lieutenant Augustus O'Hara on the road, "a spirited young officer," the first of several British leaders struck down in the bloody day's fighting. Colonel Lee also wrote that the Continental Artillery opened the duel and was under orders to withdraw the guns to the third line "as soon as the enemy should enter into close battle."[255] The cannon firing lasted about thirty minutes, after which Singleton limbered up his two pieces and retired east to the courthouse. "In this affair," wrote a rebel cavalryman, "the enemy brought the cannon to bear upon us, and their guns were so directed that the limbs of the black jack, or oak, as they are called, fell thick upon us."[256]

The British commander wasted no time once his 1,900 troops approached the Hoskins farm, "a considerable plantation." Cornwallis "resolved to attack the left of the enemy" because the woods there were more open on that flank, making troop maneuvers easier. Tarleton noted that "the troops were no sooner formed than they marched forwards with steadiness and composure" toward the rebels at the fence. Cornwallis ordered his entire army to advance in line using the road as their axis, with Tarleton's Legion still in reserve in column on the road, its colonel told "not to charge without positive orders"—perhaps with thoughts of Cowpens in the British commander's mind? As these advancing regiments struggled through the thick woods, the two units closest to the road—the 23rd on the left and the 71st on the right—reached the open fields of the Hoskins farm just over

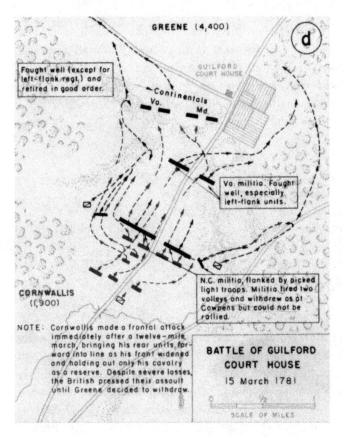

Modern map of the battle showing the movements of both armies. *West Point Atlas.*

three hundred yards from the Carolina militia line, whereas the 33rd and von Bose troops, on the far left and right of the formation, respectively, were still moving among the entangling trees.[257]

One Carolina militiaman recalled waiting "behind a rail fence, facing the cleared fields of a little farmstead. We could see down the hill about half a mile. We could see them [the British] marching along up toward that little cabin. About then our artillery guns opened up on them and the redcoats returned the fire with two guns of their own." The battle had started.[258]

The commander of Guilford County's militia recalled the scene years later as he described the enemy attack:

> *When they came [with]in about 200 yards I saw a British officer with a drawn sword driving up his men. I asked Captain [Arthur] Forbis if he could take him down. He said he could for he had a good rifle and asked me if he should shoot then. I told him to let him [with]in 50 yards and then take him down, which he did.*[259]

The British assault on Greene's first line was made with bravery and fortitude. A Loyalist witness, commissary agent Charles Stedman, observed that "the disposition being made, the [British] line received orders to advance, and moved forward with that steady and guarded, but firm and determined resolution which discipline alone can confer."[260]

Tarleton was more descriptive:

> [T]*he order and coolness of that part of Webster's brigade which advanced across the open ground* [i.e., the 23rd Regiment], *exposed to the enemy's fire, cannot be sufficiently extolled...the militia allowed the front line to approach within one hundred and fifty yards before they gave their fire... the* [British] *front line continued to move on...part of them* [the militia] *repeated their fire...the King's troops threw in their fire, and charged rapidly with their bayonets. The shock was not waited for by the militia, who retreated behind their second line* [British 1st Line].[261]

One of the Royal Welch Fusiliers (the 23rd Regiment), Sergeant Roger Lamb, later published a dramatic account of the day's early fighting. "After the brigade formed across the open ground, the colonel [Webster] rode on to the front, and gave the word, '*Charge.*' Instantly the movement was made in excellent order, in a smart run with arms charged"—that is to say, with leveled .75-caliber Brown Bess muskets and fixed bayonets. "When we arrived within forty yards of the enemy's line," Lamb stated, "it was perceived that their whole force had their arms presented [aimed], and resting on a rail fence...they were taking aim with the nicest precision." With muskets and rifles pointed directly at the oncoming British, "at this awful period a general pause took place; both parties surveyed each other for the moment with the most anxious suspense." Then Colonel Webster rode forward "in the front of the 23rd regiment, and said, with more than even his usual commanding voice (which was well known to his Brigade), '*Come on my brave Fuzileers.*' This operated like an inspiring voice, they rushed forward amidst the enemy's fire; dreadful was the havoc on both sides."[262] Another soldier of the 23rd Regiment on the field that day wrote that the redcoats attacked "under a most galling and destructive fire, which [the regiment] could only return by an occasional fire."[263]

Stedman watched the attack from the rear and wrote that "at the distance of one hundred forty yards [the British] received the enemy's first fire, but continued to advance unmoved. When arrived at a nearer and more convenient distance, they delivered their own fire, and rapidly charged with their bayonets."[264]

This assault must have been especially fearsome to most of the militia, who had few bayonets issued to them. Moreover, the militia at the fence took casualties from the redcoats' disciplined volleys, which further unnerved the amateur soldiers. For example, a Caswell County militia ensign, William Haynie, told of the bloody sites of the action. At the first line "he came past his brother John Haynie who was shot through the hips but such was the confusion and his [William's] duties that he was then performing...he could not afford him any assistance but saw him on a horse and some men carrying him out" of the battle moments later. Dozens of others were struck down as well.[265]

The official history of the Grenadier Guards recorded that "the attack of the British commenced along the whole line, and the advance, without firing, was executed with the most determined coolness, unchecked by the fire of the enemy....On approaching the Americans, the British poured in a volley and charged down upon the enemy who did not await the shock, but retired beyond their second line."[266]

On the right of the road, a Hessian saw that as his comrades advanced, the militia did not fire at them, while Major Du Buy, the von Bose Regiment's commander, observed that as the men crossed a field and scrambled over a low fence, they were not "inconvenienced by the enemy," no doubt because the militia was three hundred yards away and well out of effective smoothbore musket range. To the Germans' left, however, the Highlanders of the 71st Regiment suffered heavily as they pressed on in more open ground close to the road, receiving deadly fire from rebel riflemen laying on the ground by the fence.[267]

Before long, the assault of Cornwallis's infantry became too much for the jittery militia to face, notable in the center. Many of the Carolinians at the first line broke ranks and rushed for the rear when the British army attacked them, some never to be seen in arms again. "Like sore eyed men exposed to sunshine," Colonel Williams wrote sarcastically, the North Carolina militia "shunned the light, and abandoned a secure position behind the fence."[268] A North Carolina company officer wrote similarly that "he had the great mortification to see his men in a panic fly at the approach of the enemy, and although [he] endeavored to rally them, it was impossible, and many even retreated to their homes."[269]

General Greene harshly criticized the North Carolina militia's lack of resolve that day and blamed their unwillingness to stand firm at the fence for the army's failure to win the battle. To Congress he later reported bluntly that the British moved through the fields to attack the North Carolina brigades who

> *waited the attack until the enemy got within about one hundred forty yards, when part of them began a fire, but a considerable part left the ground without firing at all; some fired once, and some twice, and none more, except a part of a battalion of General Eaton's brigade. The general and field officers did all they could to induce the men to stand their ground, but neither the advantages of position nor any other consideration could induce them to stay. They left the ground and many of them threw away their arms.*[270]

Greene wrote to Governor Jefferson that the Carolinians "neglected to take advantage of their position, but fled, (at least the greater part of them), without giving more than one fire."[271] More specifically, he complained to George Washington that "none fired more than twice and very few more than once, and near one half not at all."[272]

After the battle, a disappointed Greene laid the blame for its outcome on these first line men. "Had the N.C. militia behaved equal to my expectation we should certainly have totally ruined the British army," he told Thomas Sumter,[273] and to North Carolina's governor, Abner Nash, he minced no words: "We ought to have had a victory, and had your militia stood by their officers it was certain."[274] Three days later, Greene's opinion had not changed. "Victory was long doubtful" through the course of the fighting, "and had the North Carolina militia done their duty it was certain." These companies "had the most advantageous position I ever saw, and left it without making scarcely the shadow of opposition…many threw away their arms and fled with the utmost precipitation, even before a gun was fired at them," although he did compliment their officers. Given Greene's long-standing criticism of using militia, he must have also been pained to think of all the arms, ammunition, equipment, and provisions he had issued to some of them before the battle, only to see hundreds of men ingloriously sprint for the rear.[275]

While it must be pointed out that Greene was not at the first line to witness the fighting there and could not see it from his headquarters, he received reports of the militia's flight and surely saw some of the refugees pouring east on the New Garden Road and through the woods to safety. Moreover, other American officers witnessed the militia's collapse. "Light-

Horse Harry" Lee recalled that "the American line, by order, began to fire" at the oncoming redcoats, but "undismayed, the British continued to advance, and having reached a proper distance, discharged their pieces and rent the air with shouts." Then came the terror, especially in the center of the rebels' line, where "to our infinite distress and mortification, the North Carolina militia took to flight, a few only of Eaton's brigade excepted."[276] And just as at Camden the summer before, "many of the officers...[tried] to stop this unaccountable panic." Lee soon "joined in the attempt to rally the fugitives, threatening to fall upon them with his cavalry. All was vain, so thoroughly confounded were these unhappy men, that, throwing away arms, knapsacks, and even canteens, they rushed like a torrent headlong through the woods."[277]

Fortunately for Greene's army, not all of the men on the first line bolted when the British host attacked. One of the militiamen recalled that "most of his company stood still till they gave four fires."[278] Another North Carolinian recalled years later the scene at the first line fence:

> *The enemy approached us and were according to the best of my belief within eighty to an hundred yards of us when they made their first fire—my recollection is that most of us stood firm until after the second fire. On the third fire there were but few if any of us left to receive it—all or nearly all had broke and retreated in great disorder.*[279]

Colonel William Campbell, on the militia's wooded left flank, wrote that as the enemy immediately moved against the fence line once deployed, some Americans fired on them. Indeed, an officer of the 71st Regiment was killed about one hundred yards in front of the militia, perhaps by a Carolina rifleman at that range. As noted earlier, several British accounts described a deadly fire coming from the fence line and the rebels' flanks.

Still, one of the chief consequences of the militia abandoning their line was that it left a large hole in the center of the Americans' advanced position, a situation not lost on the British. Lee's Legion on the left soon became isolated with Campbell's Virginian riflemen, a company of Virginia Continentals, and three North Carolina militia companies once the center of the line collapsed, even as they maintained a steady fire on the Hessians and redcoats pressing toward them. "The chasm of our order of battle, produced by this base desertion [of the militia], was extremely detrimental in its consequences," Lee bitterly recalled, and "threw the corps of Lee out of combination with the army, and also exposed it to destruction."

General Leslie ordered the 1ˢᵗ Battalion of British Guards led by Colonel Chapple Norton to move up from its reserve position, shift to the right of the Hessians, and strike the rebels in thick woods south of the road. The British general then sent the von Bose troops with the Guards after Lee's "corps of observation," which slowly retired under pressure to the rear but slightly to the south, away from the courthouse and the American forces. The combatants "imperceptivity inclined to the [British] right," creating "a kind of separate action," as Tarleton described it. Leslie's troops soon proved to be too much for Lee's men and "soon defeated everything before" them, Cornwallis proudly reported to London.[280]

Tarleton later wrote that the "thickness of the woods...prevented the cavalry making a charge" in the center so Lord Cornwallis did not think it "advisable for the British cavalry to charge the enemy" retreating on the road; instead, he sent a squadron of the British Legion dragoons led by Tarleton to reinforce Leslie's advance off to the right, the crashing musketry of which Cornwallis and his staff could clearly hear. This order was probably given just after the fighting at the second line had ended. Once the cavalry arrived at Leslie's position, Tarleton saw that the British and Hessians were "now engaged with several bodies of militia and riflemen" well south of the New Garden Road and that the Guards and von Bose "had their fair share of difficulties that day" and "could never make any decisive impression." But as the British right wing steadily fired and advanced among the trees, the hard-pressed Americans "gave ground in front" and continued to incline to their left rear. Tarleton's dragoons rescued some British prisoners in the woods during the steady close-range fighting of the infantry.[281]

Tarleton then saw an opportunity to strike: he "doubled round the right flank of the Guards, and charged with considerable effect. The enemy gave way on all sides, and were routed." Indeed, the fighting on Cornwallis's right was quite severe, and at one point, the Guards suffered severely, with many soldiers shot down, until relieved by the Hessians crashing through the brush with bayonets fixed. The Hessian commander wrote that the rifle shooting "rebels...did us much injury from behind the trees in the thick wood." At others times, the blue-coated von Bose troops found themselves surrounded and taking deadly fire, and some North Carolina militia remained on the line to engage in some fierce back-and-forth hand-to-hand fighting with the Guards. Still, Tarleton's timely mounted attack was too much to resist and pushed back the rebels, many of whom were killed or wounded by the enemy's slashing swords. One of the mounted militiamen serving under Lee later wrote of this combat. Previously shot in the fighting on New Garden Road that morning,

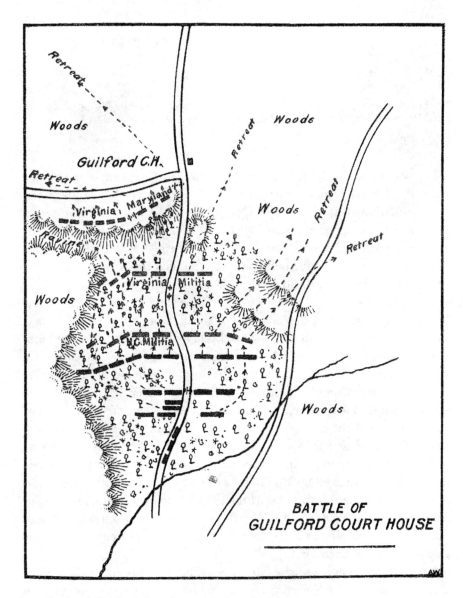

The Battle of Guilford Courthouse. *Author collection.*

later on the rebel left flank "he was wounded with a sword or cutlass across the upper part of the forehead…at the same time his horse was shot down dead, and in extricating himself, he was struck with the butt end of a musket across the right shoulder by one of the enemy and fell" but was quickly relieved by his comrades and the British soldier shot dead.[282]

An original .75-caliber Pattern 1779-S "Brown Bess" musket, carried by a soldier of the Royal Welch Fusiliers during the Revolutionary War. *Private collection.*

Lee wrote that the fighting on the American left "had long been ebbing" when the British Legion dragoons arrived; there were left "only a few resolute marksmen in the rear of Campbell, who continued firing tree to tree." A veteran stated that Colonel Campbell's Virginia riflemen on the left "did great execution in the ranks of the enemy." Stedman wrote that sharpshooters were "lurking behind trees," and their fire had no little effect. Tarleton's sudden arrival, however, inspired "these brave fellows to retire and overtake their corps." One of the riflemen wrote years later that he "received two wounds at the battle at Guilford[,] wounds…occasioned by a ball having been shot in his right leg and by a blow from a British Light horse man's sword on the left hand." In what has since been seen as a controversial decision, Lee moved his Legion to support the Continentals' third line at the courthouse while Campbell's riflemen still battled the enemy. Moreover, he apparently did so without telling Campbell, whose men suffered because of it at the hands of the enemy's dragoons. As one modern author concluded, Lee "left Campbell and his Virginians to fend for themselves" when he took his men to try to rejoin Greene's main army as it left the battlefield. Campbell, hard-pressed by Tarleton's cavalry, also managed to gather most of his command and move toward the courthouse by a circuitous route to avoid the British regulars. The Guards and Germans also moved back to Cornwallis's position along the New Garden Road at Greene's third line later in the engagement.[283]

While General Leslie's brigade struggled with Lee's Legion and Campbell's Virginians in the dense woods on the British right, Cornwallis received urgent word that his left flank too was under pressure coming from the forest beyond Webster's left regiment, the 33rd Foot. Here the redcoats came under sharp fire from Washington's corps of observation on the northern end of the first American line, including the Continental Light Dragoons, Lynch's Virginia riflemen, a North Carolina cavalry troop, and Captain Kirkwood's Delaware company. Their "heavy fire" was so effective against the oncoming 33rd Regiment that Webster had to send back to the rear for his reserve units, the Hessian Jaegers and the Guards' light infantry company, to counter Washington's threat. The 2nd Guards battalion and the Guards grenadier company also moved up to strengthen the attack to the north (left) of the road. "At this period," according to Tarleton, "the event of the action was doubtful, and victory alternatively presided over each army."[284] Eventually, Washington's flank force was pushed back by the reinforced enemy, although in an orderly fashion, having repulsed several strong attacks.[285]

Now, with the Carolina militia in flight and the two rebel flanking corps pushed back, Cornwallis's two brigades north and south of the New Garden Road went forward with little delay. Unsure of what lay ahead, British officers tried to align their jumbled units in the confusing forest in search of Greene's main line. They would soon meet a stiffer resistance a few hundred yards farther on in nearly impenetrable forested terrain, when more than one thousand well-aimed Virginia muskets and rifles gave them a deadly reception.

Chapter 13

"A Most Desperate Engagement"

The Virginians Give Way

The bursting shell, the gateway wrenched asunder,
The rattling musketry, the clashing blade;
And ever and anon, in tones of thunder,
The diapason of the cannonade.
—*Henry Wadsworth Longfellow, "The Arsenal at Springfield," 1845*

While the hard-pressed Guards and Hessians struggled on the British right flank with Lee's Legion and Campbell's deadly riflemen—a "battle within a battle," as two recent historians have aptly termed it—the rest of the redcoats pushed past Greene's abandoned first line to attack the Virginians four hundred yards farther east in a tangled forest.[286]

North of the New Garden Road, General Lawson had his men in line, bracing for the enemy's appearance just moments away. At the far right of Lawson's position were the Delaware and Virginia Continentals and Lynch's riflemen, all of whom had been pushed back by the British attack on the first line.[287]

Coming at Lawson's brigade was the 2nd Battalion of Guards along the road, and to its left (from south to north) were the Guards grenadiers, the 23rd Regiment, and the 33rd Regiment. On the 33rd's left was the Guards light infantry company and the Hessian Jaegers, groping for the end of the Americans' second position among the woods, runs, and ravines.[288]

The British infantrymen hit the rebels hard, forcing some terrified Virginians to flee their companies. The broken terrain and entangling woods,

The American army's second battle line, where the Virginia militia fought the British advance. *Author image.*

however, made it nearly impossible to maintain any semblance of order for the attackers. Instead, the combat here was one of pockets of redcoats against militia behind trees, stumps, and downed limbs, with visibility decreased by thick blue smoke from "a most tremendous fire." General Lawson himself was so close to the fighting that his horse was shot out from under him, leaving him on foot for the rest of the chaotic battle.[289]

The close-range struggle on the militia's right, noted a Virginian, was "a most desperate engagement."[290] Much of the militia held their ground for a time, and some fired as many as twenty rounds each, inflicting heavy casualties among Cornwallis's veterans as they blasted away mere yards from each other. "The Virginia militia gave the enemy a warm reception and kept up a heavy fire for a long time," wrote Greene, who heard the brisk firing from his command post at the courthouse.[291] Perhaps because the trees and dense underbrush broke up the British formations and prevented a general bayonet charge, the Virginians stood fast and bloodied Cornwallis's troops with their musketry. "They stood the fire as well as any Continental troops," a veteran stated. Fusilier Sergeant Lamb of the British 23rd Regiment recorded that "the second line of the enemy made a braver and stouter resistance than

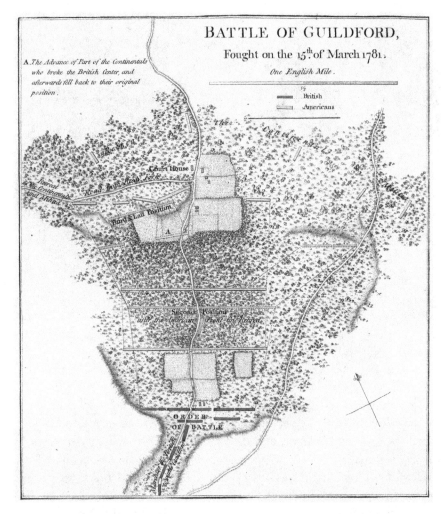

British map of the Battle of Guilford Courthouse, depicting the successive attacks on Greene's three lines beginning at the bottom of the image. *Library of Congress.*

the first. Posted in the woods, and covering themselves with trees, they kept up for a considerable time a galling fire, which did great execution."[292] After the battle, General Greene wrote that "the Virginia militia behaved nobly and annoyed the enemy greatly,"[293] and they "behaved with great gallantry." Colonel Williams also praised the Virginians, who "gave the enemy so warm a reception, and continued their opposition with such firmness…that the fate of the day was dubious for a long time."[294]

Eventually, the 23rd and the grenadiers shoved back Lawson's militia regiments from south to north with bayonets and musket volleys. Sergeant Lamb wrote that in the woods, parade ground tactics and drill "were found of little value." Instead, loading, firing, and using "the bayonet expeditiously" in close combat were far more useful.[295] Many British soldiers became low on ammunition from firing so many rounds and had to replenish their empty leather cartridge boxes from those of the dead and wounded sprawled on the damp ground around them. As Lamb was rummaging for ammunition, he was almost captured when he strayed several yards from his regiment toward enemy lines, but he managed to escape. Captain Thomas Saumarez, also of the Royal Welch Fusiliers, called his regiment's attack against the militia "cool and deliberate," which threw "the Americans into the greatest confusion." Those rebels who did not flee the dense forest were often bayoneted by the oncoming redcoats, who did not pause to reload.[296]

The grenadier company and 2nd Guards battalion were on the Fusiliers' right and closer to the road, also navigating the woods and battling with Lawson's left flank. The fighting was fierce, and several Guards officers were wounded here, including General O'Hara, who was shot in the thigh. Cornwallis reported that "the excessive thickness of the woods rendered our bayonets of little use and enabled the broken enemy to make many frequent stands with an irregular fire which occasioned some loss, and to several of the corps, great delay."[297]

Ever combative, Lord Cornwallis rode forward toward the crash of the fighting on the left. At one point, he put himself in command of the advancing Guards just north of the road "and by a vigorous charge broke the [second] line," wrote Colonel Howard of the Maryland troops.[298] The British commander, recalled Sergeant Lamb, was "mounted on a dragoon's horse," as he had already lost two horses killed under him by this point, testifying to his Lordship's proximity to the fighting. Lamb continued his account of a mounted Cornwallis at the second line, apparently unescorted by any of his staff:

> *The saddlebags were under the [horse's] belly, which much retarded his progress, owing to the vast quantity of underwood that was spread over the ground; his lordship was evidently unconscious of the danger. I immediately lay hold of the bridle of the horse and turned his head. I then mentioned to him, that if his lordship pursued in the same direction, he would in a few moments have been surrounded by the enemy, and perhaps cut to pieces or captured. I continued to run along the side of the horse, keeping the bridle in my hand, until his lordship gained the 23d regiment.*

The New Garden Road, shown here between the American first and second lines, was the axis of the British advance. *Author image.*

Such was the confusing nature of the wooded terrain, further obscured by heavy smoke.[299]

The 33rd Foot, the Hessian Jaegers, and the Guards light company far to the British left pressed on past the north end of the American second line and soon came under fire from Lynch's deadly riflemen on a thickly wooded ridge, posted there by Colonel Washington, whose dragoons and Continentals were one hundred yards to the rear. Historians Babits and Howard concluded that "some of the most terrible fighting took place along this flank." A soldier under Lynch wrote of this conflict as a "sanguinary engagement," in which he received "a severe wound in the thigh from a musket ball, which cut the main or leading sinew of his thigh." Many of Lynch's officers were killed and wounded in the fray, hit by the Jaegers' accurate, short-barreled German rifles. One of these was a Bedford County captain, who "was mortally wounded having received a ball on the left side[,] which he caught in his hand as it passed through his right side." With telling accuracy, the British light troops were eventually able to force back Lynch's men, who had no bayonets to face the oncoming redcoats. A Delaware soldier on the flank wrote that "Washington's Light Infantry behaved with almost incredible bravery, obliging the enemy to retreat in three different attacks."[300]

Soon, however, Colonel Washington's Virginia and Delaware regulars fell back to Greene's third line.[301] General Lawson's tired militia eventually fell back too, with some of the men in a panic. Two of the Virginia regiments "instantly broke off without firing a single gun and dispersed like a flock of sheep frightened by dogs," an officer observed.[302]

On the Virginians' south (left) side, General Stevens's brigade put up a stout fight in the confusing landscape, with many of the men taking up individual fighting positions. While Lee's light corps on the extreme left was pushed away from the second line by the Hessians and 1st Guards battalion, Stevens's men had to face the 71st Regiment moving rapidly against their front and at least part of the 2nd Guards battalion to his right near the New Garden Road. Cornwallis saw that "the 71st Regiment and Grenadiers and 2nd Battalion of Guards, not knowing what was passing on their right and hearing the fire advance on their left, continued to move forward, the artillery keeping pace with them on the road, followed by the cavalry."[303]

While some frightened Virginians (including the brigade major) decided to run for the rear at the approach of the fearsome highlanders coming at them as quickly as the brush and vines would allow, witness accounts show that Stevens's steady units engaged the enemy fiercely. Some of the Virginia militia even gathered tree branches and logs and piled them in front of their section of the line for defense. "The roar of the musketry and cracking of rifles were almost perpetual and as heavy as any I ever heard," declared Greene's adjutant general, Colonel Williams, about the fighting on the Virginians' front. Likewise, British commissary Stedman said that the onrushing redcoats received a "fierce and fatal fire" from the rebels.[304] Even one of the Virginia Continentals praised the second line troops: "the Virginia militia stood their ground and fought manfully."[305]

One of Stevens's two hundred Virginia militiamen from Rockbridge County, west of the Blue Ridge Mountains, was teenager Samuel Houston. He wrote that in the second line fighting, the militia and redcoats charged each other and fell back several times in the woods; at one point on Stevens's left flank, they mistook the von Bose Hessians for Continentals, due to their blue regimental coats. He fired his musket fourteen times, he recalled, indicating that the second line contest was not over quickly. Soon, however, the Rockbridge men and their comrades were struck by at least a detachment of Tarleton's

Low ground behind the American second line, across which the British advanced after defeating the Virginia militia. *Author image*.

158

dragoons. "We were obliged to run," Houston recalled, and "many were sore chased and some cut down" by the Legion cavalry's brutal swordsmen.[306]

Participant accounts indicate that many of the Virginia militiamen here fired numerous shots at the British. Once the battle lines drew close, the combat was often hand to hand, including the use of bayonets and Scottish officers' broadswords. General Stevens was wounded during this part of the action, shot through the thigh while near the road. As some of his men began to fall back once he was wounded, the injured Virginia general reluctantly ordered his section of the second line to retreat. The battered militiamen moved back quickly through the trees and across two open, grassy creek beds as the scampered for the courthouse hamlet; others joined Colonel Campbell's riflemen. "We were compelled to retreat at the top of our speed," wrote a Buckingham County militiaman, who "pulled out my cartridges[,] slipped them into my knapsack and threw the cartridge box away," trying to lighten his load. A proud Amelia soldier recalled instead that "like men & soldiers, the Virginia militia, came off with credit after having done their duty, upon that occasion and not exactly so was the case with the North Carolina militia."[307]

As the second line collapsed, the British surged ahead. "The superior discipline and bravery of the King's troops," Tarleton wrote, "again threw the militia into confusion. The thickness of the woods where these conflicts happened prevented the cavalry making a charge upon the Americans on their retreat" to the third line.[308] Nevertheless, the redcoats' "superior discipline at length prevailed and the militia were drove back upon the Continental troops" six hundred yards to the rear, Greene wrote a few days later.[309]

The bloodied rebels of Lawson's and Stevens's brigades provided a valuable service to Greene's army that cold March afternoon in the Piedmont woods, despite giving up their position. Regarding the second line combat, the battle's foremost historians concluded that "Greene's defense in depth had succeeded in breaking up the British attack formations and causing casualties. The Virginia militia had stood their ground," as had the flanking forces of Colonels Washington and Lee. Unlike the disastrous defeat at Camden the previous summer, most of the Virginia soldiers did not run from the field upon the enemy's approach.[310]

Now Greene knew, as he saw the hard-pressed Virginia militiamen drop back from their position, that the British regiments would soon come pouring out of the woods to the west, ready to decide the bloody contest for the Carolinas with one more assault. He had not long to wait.

Chapter 14

"THE SLAUGHTER WAS PRODIGIOUS"

Desperate Fighting at the Third Line

By torch and trumpet fast arrayed
Each horseman drew his battle blade,
And furious every charger neighed
To join the dreaded revelry
Then shook the hills with thunder riven,
Then rushed the steed to battle driven,
And louder than the bolts of heaven
Far flashed the red artillery
—*Thomas Campbell,* Hohenlinden, *1801*

Lord Cornwallis's winded regiments did not approach General Greene's last position simultaneously. The terrain they crossed and the opposition they faced in their attacks varied for each unit, such that the redcoats reached the western side of the low ground opposite the Continentals at different times, where they were met by the rebels' "resolution and firmness," admitted Tarleton. This favored Greene's Maryland and Virginia regulars, since not only had the Americans been recently fed and rested, but they would also not have to face the entire British army attacking at once.[311]

The edgy Continentals gripped their muskets and waited in line on the high ground just west of the Reedy Fork Road, which ran northward off the New Garden Road at the courthouse. Below and in front of the Continentals' line was a largely open hollow or vale, at the bottom of which was shallow, sandy Hunting Creek. The 2nd Maryland Regiment, led by Colonel Ford,

Hunting Creek, at the base of the ridge on which Greene posted his Continental Regiments. *Author image.*

was on the American left flank in cleared ground, its left anchored on the New Garden Road, with the courthouse a few dozen paces to its rear. To its right was Greene's best regiment, Colonel Gunby's 1st Maryland, "formed in a hollow in the wood." Colonel Williams, mounted and posted close to Greene, commanded both units of Marylanders.

To its north were the two Virginia regiments of General Huger's brigade: Colonel Hawes's 2nd Virginia and Colonel Green's 1st Virginia, joined by some of the displaced Virginia militiamen who had vacated the second line. Singleton's two brass guns were placed on the ridge just west of the road intersection, while Finley's brass cannons were situated by the Virginia troops on the right flank with a field of fire into the vale below. On the far north end of Greene's line were the already-bloodied troops of Colonel Washington's riflemen and light infantry. Behind them on the Reedy Fork Road, Washington stationed his light dragoons and the North Carolina cavalry troopers, set to gallop quickly to any threatened part of the American line.[312]

The 33rd Regiment was probably the first of the redcoat formations to crash through the forest and reach the open area, where the men faced the northernmost Virginia Continentals. General Webster, "hastening over the [second line] ground occupied by the Virginia militia, sought with zeal the Continental line, and presently approached its right wing," Colonel Lee wrote.[313] Unsupported by other troops, Webster rashly ordered the 33rd to attack across the hollow immediately, hoping to capture the two rebel cannons to his front. This was an impetuous charge against Colonel Hawes and his Virginians; perhaps Webster did not see Williams's troops on the ridge to the right or simply wanted to maintain the regiment's momentum— or was contemptuous of American regulars.

As the panting British line neared the ridge, Hawes's steady men blasted the 33rd with a massive volley from about one hundred feet away, as did the Continental guns, Kirkwood's Delaware company, and part of the 1st Maryland. Stunned by the flying lead and artillery blasts, the 33rd "was compelled to recoil from the shock" and hurry back to the woods, leaving its dead and wounded behind. "At this juncture the battle became bloody, each party making an obstinate stand," wrote a Virginia Continental.[314] Hawes's men, however, could not be induced by their shouting officers to countercharge the bloodied 33rd once it fell back and regained the top of the vale's western edge, where the soldiers had begun their assault. This "gave Webster an excellent position till he could hear of the progress of the King's troops upon his right," Tarleton noted. Webster did not have long to wait.[315]

The 2nd Battalion of Guards arrived next out of the thick woods close to the New Garden Road opposite the Maryland Continentals and Singleton's two field pieces. Perhaps pausing briefly to dress its lines on the colors, the Guards started forward with grim determination, led by General O'Hara, and ran toward the American left side with fixed bayonets. "The climactic moment of the engagement was now at hand," historians Babits and Howard concluded, for "in the next few minutes, roughly 600 fatigued and anxious men would decide the outcome of the battle of Guilford Courthouse."[316]

The surging Guards, Cornwallis wrote, were "glowing with impatience to signalize themselves." Their immediate opponent was the 2nd Maryland Regiment, posted immediately north of the road. This inexperienced regiment had only recently been raised and also lacked a proper number of experienced officers for effective discipline. At this pivotal moment, it showed. While most of the regiment's soldiers faced west, the left flank of this unit was "refused," meaning some of the soldiers were aligned back at a right angle so that they looked south and stood parallel to the New Garden Road to guard against an attack from that direction. When Colonel Ford saw the impending British assault take shape, he started to realign all of his regiment to the west to face the Guards. This seems to have caused some confusion among the raw recruits in the ranks, who were unused to maneuvering on a battlefield.

Once the entire 2nd Maryland faced west, Ford ill-advisedly ordered it to charge, a curious command given that the troops were green and his regiment occupied advantageous high ground. Colonel Williams, however, quickly ordered them back in line, having seen disorder among the puzzled men. Colonel Davie of Greene's staff, who observed the action close by, also concluded that Ford's order for the regiment to charge was the cause of great disorientation in the ranks. These troops even gave a "premature" scattered fire at the Guards, although it was ineffectual.[317]

With great enthusiasm to close with the rebels, the Guards attacked at a slow run, fired a few volleys, and then charged the 2nd Maryland. By this time, the jittery regiment had seen enough. When Colonel Ford ordered his men again to advance, "they all faced about" and ran, except for a single company.[318] The Marylanders had been routed and were pursued back to the courthouse area and beyond.

The Guards rushed forward and took as prizes Singleton's two guns, defended by a small contingent of North Carolina Continentals, who were soon overwhelmed—shot, stabbed, or captured. However, the hell-bent Guards charged with "too much ardor," said Cornwallis, and stormed well

View from Greene's third line near New Garden Road, looking downhill toward the British positions. *Author image.*

beyond the left side of the 1st Marylanders when chasing the panicked 2nd Regiment. Subsequently, they were now in the Patriots' rear, unseen by other American officers on the line due to the wooded terrain and "unevenness of the ground." The Guards' officers now recognized their fortunate situation and hurriedly turned their men around to attack the 1st Maryland, which was still facing west and unaware of the danger to its rear.[319]

Fortuitously, Colonel Gunby of the 1st Maryland received word of the Guards' threatening position from a breathless staff officer and turned about his steady regiment to face the enemy in the opposite direction. After they fired a close-range volley, Gunby's men moved toward the British and engaged them almost immediately with fixed bayonets. The fighting moved to the open ground of the vale, as multiple volleys were fired by both rebels and redcoats at very close range. Without time to reload their muskets, many soldiers on both sides had to rely solely on their bayonets instead. During the fight, Gunby's horse was killed under him, pinning the colonel to the ground; Colonel Howard, second in command, consequently assumed charge of the 1st Maryland.[320]

View of the third American line across Hunting Creek from the final British positions. *Author image.*

The fighting of the Continentals on Greene's third line at the battle of Guilford Courthouse. *U.S. Army Center of Military History.*

The sound of heavy firing could be heard clearly from Greene's opposite (right) flank. Sensing the significance of the gunfire, Colonel Washington quickly directed his horsemen south—"our own fire no doubt influenced his movement which brought him to the place where he met with the Guards," wrote Colonel Howard.[321] Washington arrived on the scene by galloping south along the Reedy Fork Road with his dragoons and two militia cavalry companies—about 120 mounted men. Unobserved by the enemy, the American dragoons smashed into rear of the unsuspecting Guards "with great slaughter," wrote Tarleton, and retook Singleton's two lost cannons as well.[322] The surging cavalry rode directly into the Guards' formation, hacking the terrified foot soldiers with swords from their mounts. The wild horsemen attacked through the disorderly Guards formation at least once more, perhaps twice. "Colonel Washington charged them so furiously that they either killed or wounded almost every man," wrote a Delaware soldier who witnessed the slaughter.[323]

One of the volunteer Virginia cavalrymen in Washington's charge was Portuguese-born Peter Francisco of Prince Edward County, a huge man of legendary size and strength, "generally known to be one of the best veterans of his day," who had fought in the Battles of Brandywine, Germantown, Stony Point, Monmouth Courthouse, and Camden; suffered at Valley Forge; and killed eleven soldiers with his sword at Guilford (it was claimed). A Virginia dragoon officer reported that "when leaving the battle ground, [Francisco] was very bloody also was his sword from point to hilt." Wounded severely in the desperate fighting by a Guard's bayonet thrust, Francisco never claimed these incredible feats, but his story became wildly embellished in later years and a monument to his heroism stands on the battleground today.[324]

After Washington's dragoons struck the Guards' rear, the Maryland infantry continued to fight the redcoats in a close-range, hand-to-hand struggle with clubbed muskets, steel bayonets, and thrusting swords. One Maryland soldier recalled bayonetting seven Guardsmen during the fighting. Another wrote that the Continentals were killing and wounding the enemy "like so many furies."[325] For example, Captain John Smith of the Marylanders narrowly avoided being stabbed by Lieutenant Colonel James Stuart, acting commander of the Guards after O'Hara's earlier wounding. When the sword-wielding Stuart stumbled and then refused to surrender, Smith gave the redcoat officer a backhand blow on the head with his own sword, killing him. Eventually, the British casualties mounted, and they were being pushed back toward the woods from which they had recently arrived.[326]

By this time, Cornwallis and his staff had arrived on the British side of the vale at the Americans' third line and observed the fighting between the Continentals and the Guards. Two field pieces under Macleod also came up on the road nearby, as did the 71st Regiment, which had been impeded by the difficult terrain and forest south of the road. The Highlanders moved toward the courthouse, to Howard's left rear, again threatening Greene's left.[327]

But down in the hollow, fighting still raged. The Guards were getting the worst of it, and the British center was threatened. Now Cornwallis ordered the artillery to fire into Washington's dragoons and the Marylanders as they attacked the Guards. The artillery fire may have inadvertently struck some nearby redcoats as well. From this incident, a myth was created decades later by Colonel Lee (who was not present on this part of the field) in his memoirs in which Cornwallis supposedly ordered the guns to fire into the confused fighting in the vale. O'Hara, having been wounded again in the fighting and lying on the ground near Cornwallis, allegedly begged him not to fire, as his own redcoats

Above: Peter Francisco's monument near the battlefield's second line commemorates his legendary service at the battle. *Author image*.

Opposite: The vale near Greene's third line, in which the Guards fought Maryland Continentals at the end of the battle. *Author image*.

would be struck down as well. Cornwallis, it was said, ordered Macleod to fire anyway to stop the American attack. As Babits and Howard deftly explained in their 2009 history of the battle, this story—told repeatedly even in modern publications—is almost certainly untrue and is not recorded by any eyewitness to the battle.[328]

When Washington withdrew his horsemen from the soft bottomland, Colonel Howard moved the 1st Maryland back to American lines. "Washington's horse having gone off," the colonel wrote, "I found it necessary to retire, which I did leisurely." As the Continentals retired, they were shot at by redcoats who had been lying on the ground but arose and fired at the Marylanders after they had passed. It was well that Howard withdrew his bloodied regiment from the low ground, as the fast-moving British now had most of their units close to Greene's third line. Moreover, O'Hara had rallied the remaining soldiers of the hard-hit 2nd Guards battalion.[329]

At some point in the action, Greene rode close to the fighting, nearly too close. He was "very near being taken[,] having rode in the heat of the action full tilt directly into the midst of the enemy," he wrote to his wife, "but by Colonel [Lewis] Morris [Jr.]" of his staff "calling to me and advertising me of my situation I had just time to retire." According to

Sluggish Hunting Creek is below the high ridge on which Greene's Virginia and Maryland Continentals waited for the British attack. *Author image.*

Henry Lee, Greene was only about thirty paces from the British before recognizing his dire predicament, although it is unclear where on the third line this incident took place.[330]

At this time, the climax of the battle had passed, although the firing continued. Riding along his lines by the Reedy Fork Road, at some point General Greene decided that staying on the field longer was too risky. Greene, Lee later wrote, was "immutable in the resolution never to risk annihilation of his force." Were he to suffer a major defeat, as Gates had at Camden, it would be next to impossible to reconstitute another southern army. He had few militia left on the field, Lee and Campbell were half a mile off to the south, ammunition was low, and one of his Continental regiments had been routed. And now Webster's troops on the British left were moving to turn Greene's right flank in the woods to the north.[331]

From his position near Huger's men, Greene had a limited view of the courthouse area and the left of his line. When he saw the soldiers of the 2nd Maryland break and run from the Guards' assault, he and other officers near him assumed that the enemy had turned the American left flank and got into their rear. He naturally feared encirclement of his army. In addition, he does not seem at first to have seen the counterattack by the 1st Maryland either, along with Washington's well-timed charge. Under mistaken assumptions, he "thought it most advisable to order a retreat," Greene later reported. Colonel Howard also recalled that after seeing the 2nd Maryland routed, the commanding general took the decision to retreat "when Ford's regiment gave way."[332]

As if to prod Greene along, Cornwallis ordered a general advance by his troops, aiming for the courthouse. On his left, Colonel Webster led the 33rd and 23rd Regiments forward and struck Hawes's Virginia regiment. The 23rd also captured both of the six-pounder field pieces on the rebel right flank. In the close fighting, Webster received a serious wound to his knee; Huger was "with his sword in his hand raised above his head encouraging his men when a shot penetrated his hand and his sword fell in his lap, which he caught up with his left, drew from his pocket a handkerchief, tied up his hand, and moved on," one of his Continentals observed. This was not a fight where senior leaders stayed to the rear.[333]

At about 3:30 p.m., the American troops began to withdraw from the third line under darkening skies. Green's Virginia regiment, having engaged in little fighting so far, covered the American retreat on the commanding general's orders. The remainder of the American army filed onto the Reedy Fork Road, headed northeast about a dozen miles to the ironworks

Right: Nathanael Greene monument at Guilford Courthouse National Military Park. *Author image.*

Below: Continental Artillery six-pounder field artillery on Greene's third lines. *Author image.*

on Troublesome Creek, which General Greene had previously designated as the place to rally in case of retreat or misfortune. While some poorly disciplined units may have become disorderly as they left the battleground pressed by the surging enemy, overall the rebels' withdrawal seems to have been made without panic; it was surely no frightened flight as at Camden. But it certainly looked like a defeat, especially to Greene. The enemy held the field, and the Rhode Island general had to leave his other two cannons and ammunition wagons in British hands by the courthouse, as all the guns' horses had been killed.

"We retreated in good order three miles," Greene later wrote to the recuperating Daniel Morgan, "and there stopped and collected our stragglers," where the road crossed Reedy Fork. Virginia officer Charles Magill wrote with pride that "never was ground contested for with greater obstinacy, and never were troops drawn off in better order." The weary, famished 23rd and 71st Regiments pursued Greene's troops briefly and halfheartedly and then returned to the battlefield exhausted. Tarleton's cavalry also chased the rebels but were repulsed several miles from the courthouse by part of Colonel Green's steady rear guard of Virginians and some militia, "who gave him so warm a reception that he retreated." A Virginia militiaman recalled that the "whole retreat was in order and… without pursuit, except some horse who showed themselves in the rear as far as the bridge over Haw River." It speaks to the intensity and duration of the day's fighting that even the Tarleton and his dragoons shied away from an aggressive chase of Greene's troops, atypical of his customary tactics.[334]

Cornwallis soon reported that the British troops "were excessively fatigued by an action which lasted an hour and a half," precluding an aggressive pursuit of the rebels. Having marched several miles since dawn without breakfast and then fought a nearly two-hour battle through rough ground and absorbing heavy casualties, the "gallant" army was simply spent. While Cornwallis rightly praised the soldiers' "very extraordinary valor," once the regiments' rolls were called and the casualties determined that evening, the demoralizing toll of battle was all too apparent. The British lost 93 killed, 413 wounded, and 26 missing, more than a quarter of Cornwallis's command. "The slaughter was prodigious" among the British ranks, "Light-Horse Harry" Lee later wrote, and they were "in no condition to advance." The officer corps was particularly hard-hit, including O'Hara, Stuart, and Webster—the latter died two weeks later and was buried in Elizabethtown, North Carolina, as the British marched slowly down the Cape Fear River.[335]

The Reedy Fork Road leads off to the right in this image and was the American army's line of retreat. The Old Salisbury Road in the foreground runs toward the British lines. *Author image.*

The American army was also bloodied in the late winter stubble fields and thick forests of Guilford County. British close-range musketry, free use of the bayonet, and hacking dragoon sabers had taken their grim toll. Although difficult to tally with certainty, the rebel losses were heavy: 79 of Greene's troops were dead on the field, and 184 were wounded, some too badly to move. Just over 1,000 men were reported missing; some of these had been captured, but far more were militiamen who had fled their positions under attack and were gone for good. Still, Greene reported to Congress that "the firmness of the officers and soldiers during the whole campaign has been almost unparalleled."[336]

To Governor Nash he wrote that "the battle was long, obstinate and bloody. We were obliged to give up the ground and lost our artillery. But the enemy have been so soundly beaten that they dare not move toward us since the action." In a flippant sentence to his friend Joseph Reid in Pennsylvania, he wrote of his army's "excessive" fatigue: "[W]e have little to eat, less to drink, and lodge in the woods in the midst of smoke."

He reported too that along Troublesome Creek the "army was in good spirits" two days after the engagement but that "the militia are leaving us in great numbers, to return home to kiss their wives and sweet hearts."[337] Word eventually arrived in Congress of the bloody engagement far to the south, a "very severe and obstinate" battle "dearly purchased owing to wholly superior discipline. One or two more such victories would ruin his Lordship," wrote a New Jersey congressman, unknowingly echoing British sentiments in the coming months.[338]

The dark evening of the battle saw no one in good spirits. Heavy, cold rain came down and drenched the suffering wounded still lying on the battle ground. A North Carolina militia soldier later testified that "he was wounded badly in the battle in the head and taken prisoner" but that seven other prisoners besides himself the night after the battle escaped from the British picket guard. Four of these brave escapees were "wounded in the attempt, and by the assistance of his comrades he reached the [American] army at the iron works" on Troublesome Creek. "The victorious troops," Colonel Lee remembered, "without tents and without food, participated in sufferings which they could not relieve."[339] Fifty terribly wounded redcoats who could not be rescued reportedly died overnight. Dozens more were eventually moved, with the American casualties as well, to nearby buildings for medical care, including the courthouse and the New Garden Friends Meeting House. Indeed, the local Quakers took in and nursed many injured soldiers regardless of the color of their regimental coats. Other American wounded soldiers were taken to Berry Hill Plantation, near South Boston, and to every nearby farm cabin or barn that could be found. A local militiaman recalled the dreadful scene: "I was on the battleground [with]in about three days after the battle was fought. The British had buried their dead and marched off. Our dead men was not all buried."[340]

Once the losses had been ascertained, it was clear that British victory had been costly. "Cornwallis undoubtedly gained a dear bought victory" wrote Major St. George Tucker of the Virginia militia while recovering from a bayonet wound. Colonel Williams concurred, writing, "I have no doubt but the enemy won [the battle] at so great an expense of blood, that the consequences would prove to him equal to a defeat." Henry Lee guessed at Cornwallis's sensations after the battle: "[N]early a third of his force slaughtered; many of his best officers killed or wounded; and that victory for which he had so long toiled and at length gained, bringing in its train not one solitary benefit." Indeed, Lee concluded years later that only the "name of victory" belonged to the decimated British, but "the substance belonged to the vanquished."[341]

The British too saw how bloody was the victory. In London, anti-administration politician Charles James Fox proclaimed in Parliament that "another such victory would ruin the British army." Charles Stedman, who saw in person the battle's terrible aftermath, later wrote that while Greene was defeated, the gruesome battle's "consequences [were] of no real advantage" to the British due to the heavy casualties they suffered. English politician Horace Walpole observed that "Lord Cornwallis has conquered his troops out of shoes and provisions and himself out of troops." This was not what King George, Lord Germain, and General Clinton expected of Cornwallis's campaign to subdue North Carolina. "Alas! That victory had every consequence of a defeat," General Clinton wrote with disgust thirteen years later.[342]

Nathanael Greene sensed immediately that the sanguinary contest was not a disaster for American arms. He called the battle "long and severe" and recognized too how badly the enemy had suffered in its "victory." He thought it "out of the enemy's power to do us any great injury," with its severe losses and still so far from resupply. "One great effort will give the enemy his death wound," he wrote hopefully to Colonel Benjamin Cleveland, a prominent backcountry North Carolina militia commander.[343]

But Greene was not to lead that "one great effort" against Cornwallis. He watched the British commander warily from Speedwell Ironworks, where he ordered his men to dig fieldworks to prepare for an enemy attack. Two days after the battle of March 15, Cornwallis had still not moved from the field, and his military intentions were unclear. Soon, however, the decimated regiments of the British army would be on the move, presenting Greene with his own strategic problems that could decide the war in the South.

Chapter 15

"Nothing but Spirit, Resolution, and Perseverance"

Aftermath

They say it was a shocking sight
After the field was won;
For many thousand bodies here
Lay rotting in the sun;
But things like that, you know, must be
After a famous victory.
—*Robert Southey, "After Blenheim," 1796*

Two days after the battle, Cornwallis drafted a proclamation to be distributed far and wide from Guilford. In it, he declared that since his troops had "totally defeated the rebel army...all friends to Great Britain are now earnestly called on to take a vigorous part," particularly the "Highlanders in Cumberland, Bladen and Anson Counties," from whom he expected supplies and loyal militia.[344] This was followed by a proclamation the next day, in which he demanded that the rebels "surrender themselves with their arms and ammunition" by April 20, and once received, they would leniently be permitted "to return to their homes upon giving a military parole and shall be protected in their persons and properties from all sort of violence from the British troops." But despite his lofty announcement that God had "crowned with signal success" his army "over the rebel forces," his Lordship was in trouble.[345]

Despite his "victory," Cornwallis's reduced army was in no condition to attack Greene at Speedwell Ironworks. The British general could not maintain his position at Guilford because local supplies were scarce, particularly flour, as the two armies had maneuvered around the area for months, consuming provisions. Badly wounded redcoats could not be moved and had to be placed in barns, homes, and churches for care. It is rarely a sign of victory for an army to leave its wounded soldiers to the care and mercy of the enemy it has purportedly just defeated.

Observed constantly by swarming American scouts, on March 18 Cornwallis decided to move his battered regiments, suffering "hunger and fatigue," south to Bell's Mill on Deep River, away from the battleground and Greene's troops. Here is where he issued his proclamation, in what he presumed to be a friendly precinct.[346] On the contrary, "many of the inhabitants rode into camp, shook me by the hand, said they were glad to see us and hear that we had beat Greene, and then rode home again." Disappointed and with "a third of my army sick and wounded...the remainder without shoes and worn down with fatigue I thought it was time to look for some place of rest and refinement." He opted to march his command southeast to Ramsey's Mill near the confluence of the Deep and Rocky Rivers (near today's Moncure), which they reached on the nineteenth, and then along the Cape Fear River by "easy marches" to Cross Creek (now Fayetteville), closer to resupply from British-held Wilmington.[347]

General Greene learned of the British withdrawal from Guilford the day they marched away. He prepared to follow the enemy but was wary of his usually combative opponent. Cornwallis "has great pride and great obstinacy and nothing but a sound beating will induce him to quit the state." Moreover, his soldiers were "good, well found, and fight with great obstinacy."[348]

To cripple the enemy as they trudged south through Tory country, Greene ordered his forces to interdict supplies going to the British, prevent Loyalist militia from mustering, and capture small enemy detachments. He began his cautious pursuit of Cornwallis by March 21, with his dragoons out front keeping an eye on the British and skirmishing all the way to Ramsey's Mill. Lee and Washington operated on the heels of the exhausted redcoats' column, with "the intention to attack the enemy."[349]

Although Greene's dogged chase of the enemy signaled a resurgence in the struggling Patriot fortunes in North Carolina, the impoverished condition of his army—although in "good spirits"—and the picked-over country through which he and the British marched prevented the American forces from striking a serious blow. "Our worthy and excellent general with his little distressed tho' successful army has in turn driven his Lordship over Cape Fear River," reported Governor Nash. The weary troops lacked almost everything, but particularly cartridges and "good beef." Supplying the southern army was still a chaotic enterprise. "The struggle here is great," he reminded Jefferson, "the situation of the army is precarious."[350]

At Ramsey's Mill, Greene's column came in sight of the redcoats, "but the river being high and rising General Greene considered it not safe to undertake to cross for the British were on the opposite bank," a Carolina militia soldier observed. One veteran recalled that "when Greene's army arrived at Ramsey Mill on Deep River No Carolina it was expected that a general engagement would ensue. A halt was ordered for the purpose of making the necessary preparation—but it was soon discovered to be merely a maneuver of Cornwallis in order to transport his baggage etc. across the river in safety."[351] A Virginia Continental remembered that "the British retreated across the river on a bridge made with fence rails, laid on the rocks, the river being shoaly at this place. They left their breakfast on the fire, which we eat, a very acceptable thing as we had eat nothing for four days and nights." Once the redcoats left, Greene's soldiers found "many of their dead[,]and a good deal of provisions such as beef &c which we ate hastily."[352]

Here a terrible scene was recalled by a Guilford County militia soldier that illustrates the brutal nature of the war in this region:

> *Whilst the army was encamped at Ramsey's Mills, there was an alarm and the army put in motion toward the point as if to meet the enemy and a hollow square formed around a tree in an open space as if to repel a charge from cavalry, when to the surprise of all, two men were conducted into the center and hung to the same limb of the tree. They... were doubtless Tories.*[353]

During his march, Lord Cornwallis received word from Major James Craig, the British commander at Wilmington since January, that it would be too difficult to supply the "destitute" army upstream on the Cape Fear. Consequently, Cornwallis continued the grueling march to Wilmington, which his famished army finally reached on April 7. "I assure you that I am quite tired of marching about the country in search of adventures," he wrote to General William Phillips in Virginia.[354]

At Ramsey's Mill, Greene also reached a momentous decision that significantly shifted the course of the war in the South. The Rhode Island general recognized that Cornwallis's force, "loaded with their wounded," would reach Wilmington within days, and there "it would be impossible for

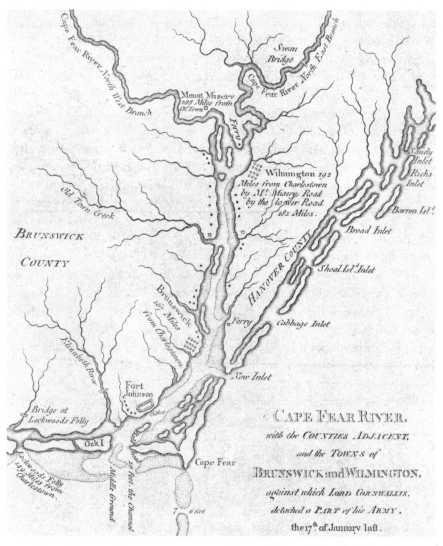

After Guilford Courthouse, Cornwallis moved to Wilmington, occupied by British forces from January to November 1781. *Library of Congress.*

us to injure them" behind their defenses and supported by navy vessels.[355] To General Washington he outlined the strategy he planned to adopt:

> *I am determined to bring the war immediately into South Carolina. The enemy will be obliged to follow us or give up their posts in that state. If the former takes place it will draw the war out of* [North Carolina] *and give*

it an opportunity to raise its proportion of men. If they leave their posts to fall they must lose more there than they can gain here. If we continue in this state the enemy will hold their positions in both. All things considered I think the movement is warranted by the soundest reasons both political and military. The maneuver will be critical and dangerous.

This plan was risky, as it would leave Cornwallis in the Patriots' rear once he took up a position in South Carolina. To Major Burnet of his staff he explained that in South Carolina the "enemy now have almost entire command of the supplies of the state and by going there we shall be able to share it with them at least." Still, he was violating a long-held military maxim that a commander should not leave an enemy force in the rear. But Greene had risked disaster just after he assumed command at Charlotte when he divided his force; now, he would take his chances again. "Don't be surprised if my movements don't correspond to your ideas of military propriety," he wrote to a militia officer. Greene expected to move south in early April, with the expectation that Cornwallis would follow him. He also hoped to cooperate with South Carolina militia forces, particularly those led by General Sumter. Concluding his letter to Washington, he wrote, "I shall take every measure to avoid a misfortune." Colonel Lee's Legion was the first of Greene's units to begin the march into South Carolina on April 5; by April 19, his army had reached a position just north of Camden, still occupied by British forces.[356]

At Wilmington, Cornwallis also had to decide on a course of action. Tarleton noted that once at the river port town, British forces started to refit, and Cornwallis "prepared his public dispatches for the minister [Germain], and meditated the future operations of his army." Writing to Clinton for the first time in weeks, he outlined his intentions to bring the war to Virginia:

I am very anxious to receive your Excellency's commands, being as yet totally in the dark, as to the intended operations of the summer. I cannot help expressing my wishes, that the Chesapeake may become the seat of war, even (if necessary) at the expence of abandoning New York. Until Virginia is in a manner subdued, our hold of the Carolinas must be difficult, if not precarious. The rivers of Virginia are advantageous to an invading Army, but North Carolina is, of all the provinces in America, the most difficult to attack, (unless material assistance could be got from the inhabitants, the contrary of which I have sufficiently experienced) on account of the great extent of the numberless rivers and creeks, & the total want of interior navigation.[357]

Without bothering to wait for Clinton's reply, Lord Cornwallis made a decision on his own for the next campaign. With the surviving veterans of Guilford Courthouse, he marched north to subdue the Old Dominion, trying to crush the Patriots' ability to sustain the war in the South by crippling their logistical base. In operations that spanned widely from Petersburg to Hanover and from Charlottesville to Portsmouth, Cornwallis and his small army ranged across the Old Dominion against the Marquis de Lafayette from May to September, but ultimately they came to ruin at the small port of Yorktown in October 1781.

After moving away from Cornwallis and into South Carolina, General Greene and his troops endured two more years of deprivation, illness, near starvation, and fighting until 1783. Victory eluded them in three major South Carolina battles: at Hobkirk Hill, the Siege of Ninety Six, and at Eutaw Springs. Despite these reverses, after each battle the British soon retreated. "We fight, get beat, rise, and fight again," Greene famously quipped, no doubt thinking of his 1781 winter campaign in North Carolina when he wrote it. The Rhode Island general eventually persevered with his troops until the enemy evacuated Charleston in 1783. But Greene's tumultuous journey to ultimate victory in the South started more than two years earlier in the bare, late winter woods and barren fields around Guilford Courthouse.

THE BATTLE OF GUILFORD Courthouse was one of the most remarkable engagements of the Revolutionary War. This was true from strategic, tactical, and command perspective. Moreover, the battle's results were unusually decisive, not just for the 1781 campaign but for the war's overall result as well.

The action of March 15, 1781, was the crucial turning point of the British southern campaign starting in 1778 and was thus a watershed event from a strategic standpoint—that is, the gaining of overall or long-term military advantage for one army or the other. Prior to the conflict at Guilford, British forces and their Loyalist allies had largely succeeded militarily (though not always politically), in that they had been victorious in almost all of the southern battles going back to the taking of Savannah in 1778. They had also defended the city against Lincoln's rebels and d'Estaing's French forces the next year, successfully laid siege to Charleston in 1780, and routed Gates's army at Camden, which became their backcountry base. By the end of 1780, they also occupied key posts at Ninety Six, Cheraw, and Georgetown, along with coastal Georgia. While it was true that Patriot forces won impressive victories in upcountry South Carolina at Musgrove Mill, Kings Mountain, and Cowpens by the middle of January 1781, these American successes were not decisive, in that they did not prevent an offensively minded Cornwallis from invading North Carolina, his objective.

Getting back the initiative after Tarleton's defeat at Cowpens, the British were able to take Charlotte, beat the rebels at Cowan's Ford, and chase Greene and his command out of North Carolina by mid-February. Once at Hillsborough, Cornwallis could claim to have conquered a large part of the state, and if supplies could be had from the coast by riverine transportation—granted, a difficult logistical challenge—success looked promising.

But the outcome of the Battle of Guilford Courthouse considerably changed this strategic setting. Although the British defeated Greene and held the field, their momentum was stopped. Cornwallis's weary soldiers could not chase the rebels to follow up the victory, no armed Loyalists rushed into British camps to join the "victors," and within three days the British army turned away from Greene's camps. They could no longer continue and had to retreat. They marched south for much hoped-for relief at Cross Creek and Wilmington, which was now a demonstration of despair, no longer an invasion. Their heavy battle casualties, especially among the officers, and tightening supply difficulties meant that Cornwallis's campaign was spent like a dropping flare, and his strategy had failed. When in April Cornwallis marched north to Petersburg, which he reached in May, North Carolina was free of all redcoats except for the small detachment at Wilmington. This was directly the result of his ruinous victory at Guilford Courthouse.

On the contrary, while Greene had been bested and many militiamen set off for home right after the battle, he still had an army in the field. His troops could chase after the redcoats, gather supplies, and give a thrashing to local Tories who grew too bold. Probably nothing better illustrates the changed strategic situation after the battle at Guilford than what each army did upon reaching Ramsey's Mill along the Deep River: the British limped on to Wilmington for succor, while Greene was free to move in to South Carolina for a new campaign.

From a tactical viewpoint, how the battle was fought was also noteworthy. Cornwallis's attack of Greene's three lines was head-on like at Camden, without any flanking maneuvers or an attempt to have Tarleton's cavalry get into the rear of Greene's army. In part, the wooded terrain dictated what the troops could do, but perhaps the British commander also sought to overawe the rebel militia with a bold bayonet charge to panic them into a retreat. If so, it worked.

But once the surging British regiments got past the rail fence and faced the two Virginia brigades, they ran into the inherent effectiveness of Greene's deployment. Not only were these militiamen experienced—some had seen prior Continental service—but they were also posted in entangling brush and trees, which broke up British formations and limited bayonet charges. The Virginians also did not give way at first, and many fired more than a dozen times before finally forced to quit their line. Greene's defense in depth worked well, such that once the British got to the final American position, they faced unbloodied Continentals.

British officers who reached the third line must have been surprised at the resistance they faced there. They saw a line of hundreds of Continentals and four field guns, all set on a ridge awaiting an attack. This was not at all like Gates's faulty deployment at Camden, Robert Howe's frightened troops at Savannah, or other northern battles some of the scarlet-clad officers had experienced earlier in the war. First, Colonel Webster's bayonet charge against Huger's Continentals was quickly repulsed. But arguably the most astonishing moment of the battle came on Greene's left flank among the Marylanders and the Continental dragoons. Despite the 2nd Maryland's terrified flight once attacked by the Guards, the 1st Maryland veterans did not panic; instead, they had the cool courage and training to face about, fire at the Guards, and attack. The fighting was close-up and bloody and saw the soldiers of both sides plunge their bayonets into enemies mere feet away. The long-held desire by Greene, von Steuben, Washington, and others American generals for competent regular troops in American uniforms was a reality at Guilford Courthouse.

Colonel Washington's astute recognition of the battle's escalation on the left and his well-executed cavalry charge into the unsuspecting Guards was also demonstrative of the tactical acuity of the Continental officers. Perhaps Tarleton showed the highest respect for Greene's soldiers when he ended his pursuit of the rebels down Reedy Fork Road after just three miles he faced Virginia Continentals with loaded muskets at the ready, poised to secure the retreat route.

The fight at Guilford Courthouse also showed Washington and Congress that they were right to have sent Greene to command the Southern Department the previous year. Not only did Greene take sound advice from Morgan on how to position his troops, but his other actions around the time of the battle also proved his leadership acumen. As noted earlier, the general knew when to be wary of the British and when to bring his force closer; he sent forward his light troops to watch the enemy so they could avoid surprises; designated in advance a location at Speedwell Ironworks for the army to reach in case of defeat; and prearranged for the collection of boats at key river crossings while denying them to his foe.

Greene's decision to retreat from the battleground also showed mature generalship. It is unknown exactly when he decided to withdraw his army, although it is likely that once he knew of the 2nd Maryland's headlong flight and the Guards in the rear, the decision was obvious.[358] No doubt he was also influenced by the arrival at the vale of all of the British units. It would have been tempting to stay on the third line's ridge to finish the fight, especially with the success his troops had already shown. But Greene was a prudent commander, a skill he surely learned from more than five years of service with General Washington. The core of his army was mostly intact, just one of his regular regiments had panicked, and he had a secure line of retreat to the north. Conscious that he had more to lose by staying and suffering defeat than moving off with an army that could fight another day, he wisely chose the latter.

Looking back four decades later, Thomas Jefferson recalled Greene's value to the American cause, due in part to decisions like those he took while campaigning against Cornwallis. The elderly "sage of Monticello" wrote that Greene was "second to no one in enterprise, in resource, in sound judgment, promptitude of decision, and every other military talent."[359]

In a letter to North Carolina militia leader Colonel Alexander Lillington on March 29, 1781, from Ramsey's Mill, Greene implored him to stay out of danger, watch Cornwallis's long column heading for Wilmington, remove supplies the redcoats could seize, and take away all horses, which were badly needed by the British. "Little by little we shall reduce the British," he wrote, "and nothing but spirit, resolution, and perseverance are necessary for this purpose." Surely no one in the southern theater exemplified these essential traits more than the Rhode Island General Nathanael Greene.[360]

NOTES

Introduction

1. Nathanael Greene to Thomas Jefferson, March 16, 1781, Boyd et al., *Papers of Thomas Jefferson* (hereafter *Jefferson Papers*), 5:156–57.

Prologue

2. George Washington to George Clinton, September 26, 1780, Founders Online, National Archives.
3. "General Greene's Orders," October 7, 1780, Showman and Conrad et al., *Papers of General Nathanael Greene* (hereafter *Greene Papers*), 6:350–51; Greene to George Washington, October 8, 1780, *Greene Papers*, 6:356; Greene to George Clinton, October 9, 1780, *Greene Papers*, 6:360.
4. George Washington to Nathanael Greene, October 14, 1780, *Greene Papers*, 6:385–87.
5. Maass, *Horatio Gates and the Battle of Camden*.
6. Greene to Jeremiah Wadsworth, October 15, 1780, *Greene Papers*, 6:391–92.
7. Greene to George Washington, October 16, 1780, *Greene Papers*, 6:396.
8. Greene to Catherine Greene, October 16, 1780, *Greene Papers*, 6:398; Greene to Jeremiah Wadsworth, October 15, 1780, *Greene Papers*, 6:391–92.
9. Greene to George Washington, April 22, 1779, *Greene Papers*, 3:423.
10. Greene to John Mathews, October 3, 1780, *Greene Papers*, 6:335–36.

11. Greene to George Washington, October 16, 1780, *Greene Papers*, 6:396.

12. Greene to William Greene, October 19, 1780, *Greene Papers*, 6:411.

13. Greene to Hugh Hughes, October 17, 1780, *Greene Papers*, 6:402–3; Greene to Catherine Greene, October 21, 1780, *Greene Papers*, 6:415–16.

Chapter 1

14. Shachtman, *How the French Saved America*, 114–15.

15. Martin and Preston, *Theaters of the American Revolution*, 90; Rauch, "Southern Discomfort," 34–50.

16. Weddle, "Change of Both Men and Measures," 837–65.

17. Willcox, *Portrait of a General*, 208. Clinton assumed command in May once General Howe left Philadelphia to return to England.

18. O'Shaughnessy, *Men Who Lost America*, 215.

19. Willcox, *Portrait of a General*, 3–39.

20. O'Shaughnessy, *Men Who Lost America*, 213–14.

21. Willcox, *Portrait of a General*, 211; O'Shaughnessy, *Men Who Lost America*, 210; "Treaty of Alliance with France," 1778, Primary Documents in American History, Library of Congress, http://www.loc.gov/rr/program/bib/ourdocs/alliance.html; Shachtman, *How the French Saved America*, 130.

22. Shachtman, *How the French Saved America*, 130.

23. Weddle, "Change of Both Men and Measures," 859–62.

24. O'Shaughnessy, *Men Who Lost America*, 212, 221; Martin and Preston, *Theaters of the American Revolution*, 78–79.

25. Martin and Preston, *Theaters of the American Revolution*, 90; Willcox, *Portrait of a General*, 263, 293; O'Shaughnessy, *Men Who Lost America*, 213; Edward Lengel and Mark Lender in *Theaters of the American Revolution*, 56–57.

26. Lefler and Newsome, *North Carolina*, 77–81; Rauch, "Southern Discomfort," 34–50; Weddle, "Change of Both Men and Measures," 857.

27. Piecuch, *Three Peoples, One King*, 4–6; Weddle, "Change of Both Men and Measures," 857.

28. O'Shaughnessy, *Men Who Lost America*, 223; Martin and Preston, *Theaters of the American Revolution*, 106.

29. Wilson, *Southern Strategy*, 65–80.

30. Martin and Preston, *Theaters of the American Revolution*, 107.

31. Taffee, *Philadelphia Campaign*, 2.

32. Wilson, *Southern Strategy*, 81–99; Pancake, *This Destructive War*, 32–33.

33. John C. Cavanaugh, "American Military Leadership in the Southern Campaign: Benjamin Lincoln," in Higgins, *Revolutionary War in the South*, 101–32; Pancake, *This Destructive War*, 33; Piecuch, *Three Peoples, One King*, 129–31.
34. Wilson, *Southern Strategy*, 133–81; Willcox, *Portrait of a General*, 293.
35. Martin and Preston, *Theaters of the American Revolution*, 115–16; George Washington to James Bowdoin, June 14, 1780, Founders Online, National Archives; Benjamin Lincoln to George Washington, June 25, 1780, Founders Online, National Archives. The definitive work on this siege is Borick, *Gallant Defense*.
36. Washington to Jonathan Trumbull Sr., June 11, 1780, Founders Online, National Archives.
37. Washington to James Bowdoin, June 14, 1780, Founders Online, National Archives.

Chapter 2

38. Billias, *George Washington's Generals*, 203.
39. Martin and Preston, *Theaters of the American Revolution*, 119; Pancake, *This Destructive War*, 69.
40. Pancake, *This Destructive War*, 70; Willcox, *Portrait of a General*, 321; O'Shaughnessy, *Men Who Lost America*, 231.
41. Martin and Preston, *Theaters of the American Revolution*, 117–18; Pancake, *This Destructive War*, 69–70; O'Shaughnessy, *Men Who Lost America*, 232.
42. O'Shaughnessy, *Men Who Lost America*, 249–50.
43. Ibid., 250–51.
44. Ibid., 253–54.
45. Ibid., 254–55.
46. Willcox, *Portrait of a General*, 314–19; O'Shaughnessy, *Men Who Lost America*, 255–56.
47. Willcox, *Portrait of a General*, 319–20.
48. Clinton to Cornwallis, May 20, 1780, Clark, *Colonial and State Records of North Carolina*, 15:244 (hereafter *CSRNC*); Piecuch, *Three Peoples, One King*, 184; Willcox, *Portrait of a General*, 320; Pancake, *This Destructive War*, 68.
49. Pancake, *This Destructive War*, 69.
50. Schellhammer, "Tarleton." See also Scotti, *Brutal Virtue*.
51. Pancake, *This Destructive War*, 64.

52. Borick, *Gallant Defense*, 193.

53. Jim Piecuch, "Massacre or Myth? Banastre Tarleton at the Waxhaws, May 29, 1780," in *Compendium of Research Materials on The Battle of the Waxhaws, May 29, 1780*, comp. Charles B. Baxley (2004), 7 (in author's collection); Scoggins, *Day It Rained Militia*, 46

54. Greene to Samuel Huntington, December 28, 1780, *Greene Papers*, 7:9; Pancake, *This Destructive War*, 71–72; Thomas Burke to James Craig, June 29, 1781, *CSRNC*, 15:49–55.

Chapter 3

55. Samuel Huntington to Horatio Gates, June 13, 1780, in Smith, *Letters of Delegates to Congress*, 15:312.

56. George A. Billias, "Horatio Gates, Professional Soldier," in *Washington's Generals*, 79, 96, 99.

57. Lengel, *General George Washington*, 264.

58. Ibid., 264–65.

59. John Armstrong Sr. to Horatio Gates, June 15, 1780, in Smith, *Letters of Delegates*, 15:319.

60. Horatio Gates to Benjamin Lincoln, July 4, 1780, in Stevens, "Southern Campaign," 283; Horatio Gates to Director of Hospitals, July 19, 1780, in Stevens, "Southern Campaign," 284.

61. Gates to Jefferson, July 19, 1780, Founders Online, National Archives.

62. Horatio Gates to Thomas Jefferson, August 3, 1780, Founders Online, National Archives; Gates to Caswell, July 25, 1780, in Stevens, "Southern Campaign," 292; Paul David Nelson, "Major General Horatio Gates as a Military Leader: The Southern Experience," in Higgins, *Revolutionary War in the South*, 135.

63. Piecuch, *Battle of Camden*, 40–41; Smith, *Camden 1780*, 13, 66.

64. Robert R. Livingston to John Jay, August 26, 1780, in Smith, *Letters of Delegates*, 15:623.

65. Piecuch, *Battle of Camden*, 37–39.

66. Otho Hollins Williams to Alexander Hamilton, August 30, 1780, *Papers of Alexander Hamilton*, 2:387.

67. Piecuch, *Battle of Camden*, 44.

68. "Field return of the troops under the command of Lieutenant-general Earl Cornwallis, on the night of the 15th of August, 1780," in Tarleton, *History of the Campaigns*, 136.

69. Gates to Samuel Huntington, August 20, 1780, in Stevens, "Southern Campaign," 302–3.

70. Piecuch, *Battle of Camden*, 41–42.

71. Josiah Martin to Lord George Germain, August 18, 1780, *CSRNC*, 15:49–55.

72. Gates to Samuel Huntington, August 20, 1780, in Stevens, "Southern Campaign," 302–3.

73. Pancake, *This Destructive War*, 105–7; Nelson, "Gates as a Military Leader," 146–47; Gates to Samuel Huntington, August 20, 1780, in Stevens, "Southern Campaign," 304–5; Piecuch, *Battle of Camden*, 45.

74. Pancake, *This Destructive War*, 107; Martin to Germain, August 18, 1780, *CSRNC*, 15:49–55. This small battle was fought just north of today's Great Falls, South Carolina.

75. John Henry to Thomas S. Lee, September 2, 1780, in Smith, *Letters of Delegates*, 16:9; Samuel Huntington to Jonathan Trumbull Sr., September 4, 1780, in Smith, *Letters of Delegates*, 16:16; Samuel Huntington to Horatio Gates, September 9, 1780, in Smith, *Letters of Delegates*, 16:42.

76. Gates to Le Chevallier La Luzerne, August 28, 1780, in Stevens, "Southern Campaign," 306–7.

77. Gates to Samuel Huntington, August 20, 1780, in Stevens, "Southern Campaign," 304–5; Gates to William Smallwood, August 24, 1780, in Stevens, "Southern Campaign"; Documentary History of the Battle of Camden, http://www.battleofcamden.org/jstevens.htm.

78. Gates to Washington, August 30, 1780, Founders Online, National Archives; North Carolina State Senate resolution, August 31, 1780, General Assembly Session Records, August/September 1780, North Carolina State Archives.

Chapter 4

79. Gates to Caswell, August 22, 1780, in Stevens, "Southern Campaign," 304–5.

80. Gates to Washington, August 30, 1780, in Stevens, "Southern Campaign," 309.

81. Willie Jones to Abner Nash, October 1, 1789, in Smith, *Letters of Delegates*, 16:122.

82. John Hanson to Thomas S. Lee, September 11, 1780, in Smith, *Letters of Delegates*, 16:51.

83. John Hanson to Philip Thomas, September 19, 1780, in Smith, *Letters of Delegates*, 16:92.

84. Daniel of St. Thomas Jennifer to Thomas S. Lee, October 2, 1780, in Smith, *Letters of Delegates*, 16:130.

85. Samuel Huntington to Washington, October 6, 1780, in Smith, *Letters of Delegates*, 16:154.

86. John Mathews to Washington, October 6, 1780, in Smith, *Letters of Delegates*, 16:159; John Mathews to Washington, October 17, 1780, in Smith, *Letters of Delegates*, 16:218–19; Nathaniel Peabody to Richard Henry Lee, October 27, 1780, in Smith, *Letters of Delegates*, 16:281; John Hanson to Charles Carroll, October 30, 1780, in Smith, *Letters of Delegates*, 16:284.

87. Gates to Washington, September 3, 1780, *CSRNC*, 15:65–66.

88. Horatio Gates to Jethro Sumner, September 19, 1780, *CSRNC*, 14:773; Horatio Gates to Jethro Sumner, September 30, 1780, *CSRNC*, 14:778–79.

89. Smallwood to Gates, August 31, 1780, *CSRNC*, 14:580–82; Smallwood to Gates, September 2, 1780, *CSRNC*, 14:587; Ralph Falkner to Horatio Gates, September 25, 1780, *CSRNC*, 14:648–49; Sumner to Gates, September 3, 1780, *CSRNC*, 14:590; Memorandum from Otho Holland Williams and Benjamin Ford, September 8, 1780, *CSRNC*, 14:604.

90. Sumner to Gates, September 15, 1780, *CSRNC*, 14:616.

91. "Biographical Sketch of Thomas Polk," *CSRNC*, 15:178; Gates to Thomas Polk, December 9, 1780, *Greene Papers*, 6:558–59.

92. Thomas Polk to Gates, September 10, 1780, *CSRNC*, 14:606.

93. "Resolution by North Carolina Concerning the Defense of the State of North Carolina," General Assembly, September 13, 1780, *CSRNC*, 14:612–13.

94. Lathan, "We Are Family"; "Report by the United States Senate Concerning William Lee Davidson's Military Service in the Revolutionary War," January 21, 1857, *CSRNC*, 22:118–20.

95. A full-length biography of Davie is Robinson, *William R. Davie*.

96. William Lee Davidson to Gates, September 14, 1780, *CSRNC*, 14:614–15; Davidson to Gates, September 14, 1780, *CSRNC*, 14:615–16; Sumner to Gates, September 24, 1780, *CSRNC*, 14:646–48.

97. Jethro Sumner to Horatio Gates, September 25, 1780, *CSRNC*, 14:651.

Chapter 5

98. Cornwallis to Germain, August 21, 1780, *CSRNC*, 15:268–73.

99. Cornwallis to Clinton, August 23, 1780, *CSRNC*, 15:273–76; Maass, *Road to Yorktown*, 25–27.

100. North Carolina Delegates to the North Carolina Council of Safety, February 13, 1776, in Smith, *Letters of Delegates*, 3:250–51; Petition of Samuel Hawkins et al., April 10, 1782, *CSRNC*, 16:276–77.

101. Cornwallis to Clinton, August 23, 1780, *CSRNC*, 15:273–76.

102. Ibid.

103. Cornwallis to Clinton, August 29, 1780, *CSRNC*, 15:276–78; see also Lee, *Crowds and Soldiers*.

104. Cornwallis to Lord George Germain, September 19, 1780, *CSRNC*, 15:278–82.

105. Cornwallis to Clinton, August 29, 1780, *CSRNC*, 15:276–78.

106. Ibid.

107. Ibid.

108. Ibid.; O'Shaughnessy, *Men Who Lost America*, 263.

109. Saberton, "Cornwallis and the Autumn Campaign."

110. Ibid.

111. Cornwallis to Germain, September 19, 1780, *CSRNC*, 15:278–82.

112. Cornwallis to Clinton, September 22, 1780, *CSRNC*, 15:282.

113. Stevens, *Campaign in Virginia*, 1:65.

114. Saberton, "Cornwallis and the Autumn Campaign."

115. Seawell to Sumner, September 25, 1780, *CSRNC*, 14:776–77; Stedman, *History of the Origins, Progress, and Termination*, 2:216; Pension Application of Henry Connelly, W8188, fn106NC, www.southerncampaign.org.

116. Saberton, "Cornwallis and the Autumn Campaign."

117. O'Shaughnessy, *Men Who Lost America*, 263.

118. Patten, "Ferguson and His Rifle."

119. O'Shaughnessy, *Men Who Lost America*, 263.

120. Thomas Polk to Horatio Gates, September 11, 1780, *CSRNC*, 14:608–9.

121. William Lee Davidson to Horatio Gates, October 6, 1780, *CSRNC*, 14:674–75.

122. William Campbell to Arthur Campbell, October 20, 1780, Draper, *King's Mountain and Its Heroes*, 526.

Chapter 6

123. Cornwallis to Clinton, December 3, 1780, *CSRNC*, 15:302–7; Cornwallis to Alexander Leslie, November 12, 1780, *CSRNC*, 15:298–300.

124. Gates to Jefferson, November 3, 1780, *Jefferson Papers*, 4:91–92.

125. Gates to Jefferson, October 20, 1780, *Jefferson Papers*, 4:49–50.

126. Cornwallis to Clinton, December 3, 1780, in Saberton, *Cornwallis Papers*, 3:24–27 (hereafter "*Cornwallis Papers*").

127. Ibid.

128. "Order from Horatio Gates Concerning the Transfer of Command of the Southern Department of the Continental Army," December 3, 1780, *CSRNC*, 15:170; Greene's Orders, December 5, 1780, *Greene Papers*, 6:527.

129. Gates to Washington, January 15, 1781 (with enclosures), Founders Online, National Archives; Gates to Washington, May 22, 1781, Founders Online, National Archives; Billias, *George Washington's Generals and Opponents*, 103. Gates's home, Traveler's Rest, is located in what is now Jefferson County, West Virginia.

130. Greene to Washington, April 24, 1779, *Greene Papers*, 3:427. See also Morgan, "Nathanael Greene as Quartermaster General." Greene left the Quakers formally in 1777.

131. *Greene Papers*, 1:xvi–xix; Tucker, *Rise and Fight Again*, 2–8.

132. For modern biographies of Greene see Golway, *Washington's General*, and Carbone, *Nathanael Greene*.

133. Washington to Greene, October 22, 1780, *Greene Papers*, 6:424–25.

134. Greene to Alexander McDougal, October 30, 1780, *Greene Papers*, 6:446–47; Greene to Henry Knox, October 29, 1780, *Greene Papers*, 6:442.

135. Greene to Washington, October 31, 1780, *Greene Papers*, 6:447–49.

136. Greene to the Board of War, November 7, 1780, *Greene Papers*, 6:468; Greene to Thomas Sim Lee, November 10, 1780, *Greene Papers*, 6:473.

137. Greene to Washington, November 13, 1780, *Greene Papers*, 6:478; Greene to Washington, November 19, 1780, *Greene Papers*, 6:485.

138. Greene to Washington, November 19, 1780, *Greene Papers*, 6:485–87; Greene to Washington, November 19, 1780, *Greene Papers*, 6:488–89.

139. For Jefferson's difficult two years as governor, see Maass, *Road to Yorktown*.

140. Greene to Jefferson, November 20, 1780, *Greene Papers*, 6:491–93.

Chapter 7

141. *Greene Papers*, 6:xvii.
142. Greene to Nash, December 6, 1780, *Greene Papers*, 6:533–34.
143. Greene to Jefferson, December 6, 1780, *Greene Papers*, 6:530.
144. Ibid.
145. Greene to North Carolina Board of War, December 7, 1780, *Greene Papers*, 6:548–49.
146. Edward Stevens to Jefferson, August 27, 1780, *Jefferson Papers*, 3:563; Nash to Samuel Huntington, October 6, 1780, *CSRNC*, 15:98–99.
147. Greene to Catherine Greene, December 7, 1780, *Greene Papers*, 6:542.
148. Greene to Washington, December 7, 1780, *Greene Papers*, 6:543.
149. Seymour, "Journal of the Southern Expedition," 286–98, 377–94 (quote is on page 292); Greene to Samuel Huntington, December 28, 1780, *Greene Papers*, 7:8.
150. Greene to Jefferson, December 6, 1780, *Greene Papers*, 6:531.
151. Greene to Stevens, December 1, 1780, *Greene Papers*, 6:512–14; Greene to Kosciuszko, December 3, 1780, *Greene Papers*, 6:515; Greene to Carrington, December 4, 1780, *Greene Papers*, 6:516–17. Taylor's Ferry was located near modern Boydton.
152. Greene to Carrington, December 4, 1780, *Greene Papers*, 6:516.
153. Greene to North Carolina Board of War, December 7, 1780, *Greene Papers*, 6:548–49; Greene to Robert Gillies, January 9, 1781, *Greene Papers*, 7:83.
154. Sam Fore, "William Pierce (1753–1789)," New Georgia Encyclopedia, https://www.georgiaencyclopedia.org/articles/history-archaeology/william-pierce-1753-1789.
155. Greene to William R. Davie, December 11, 1780, *Greene Papers*, 6:561–62; Robinson, *Revolutionary War Sketches*.
156. Boatner, *Encyclopedia of the American Revolution*, 1,208–9; O'Donnell, *Washington's Immortals*, 246, 268–69.
157. Buchanan, *Road to Guilford Courthouse*, 276–88; Babits, *Devil of a Whipping*, 23–24. See also Zambone, *Daniel Morgan*.
158. Troop figures are given in Buchanan, *Road to Guilford Courthouse*, 288, but no source is given for the returns. See also Babits, *Devil of a Whipping*, 23–28; Greene to Washington, December 9, 1780, *Greene Papers*, 6:559–60; Boatner, *Encyclopedia of the American Revolution*, 1,018; Anderson, "William Washington," 1821; Pension Application of William Hill, R5016, www.southerncampaign.org.

159. O'Donnell, *Washington's Immortals*, 276; Boatner, *Encyclopedia of the American Revolution*, 1,019; Dennis Conrad's quote about the legion is in Massey and Piecuch, *General Nathanael Greene*, 10. Henry Lee would become the father of Confederate general Robert E. Lee.

160. General William Bryan to Richard Caswell, April 27, 1779, *CSRNC*, 14:74–75; Greene to Alexander Hamilton, January 10, 1781, *Greene Papers*, 7:87–91; Greene to Jacob Greene (?), September 28, 1776, *Greene Papers*, 1:303; Greene to Lewis Morris, September 14, 1780, *Greene Papers*, 6:284; Greene to Joseph Reed, September 5, 1780, *Greene Papers*, 6:260–61; Greene to Joseph Reed, September 19, 1780, *Greene Papers*, 6:296; Greene to Nathaniel Peabody, September 6, 1780, *Greene Papers*, 6:267; Zambone, *Daniel Morgan*, 210.

161. Greene to Nathaniel Peabody, December 8, 1780, *Greene Papers*, 6:554.

162. Greene to Nash, December 6, 1780, *Greene Papers*, 6:533–34; Greene to North Carolina Board of War, December 7, 1780, *Greene Papers*, 6:548–49. The board was abolished in January 1781.

163. Greene to Francis Marion, December 4, 1780, *Greene Papers*, 6:519–20.

Chapter 8

164. Greene to North Carolina Board of War, December 14, 1780, *Greene Papers*, 6:574–75.

165. Greene to Daniel Morgan, December 16, 1780, *Greene Papers*, 6:589; Greene to Samuel Huntington, December 28, 1780, *Greene Papers*, 7:7; Stevens to Jefferson, January 24, 1781, Founders Online, National Archives; Ichabod Burnet to unknown, January 23, 1781, South Caroliniana Library, University of South Carolina; Greene to Marquis de Lafayette, December 29, 1780, *Greene Papers*, 7:18–19; Babits, *Devil of a Whipping*, 7–9. Greene's camp was near modern Wallace, South Carolina, along Hick's Creek.

166. Scheer and Rankin, *Rebels and Redcoats*, 425–26; Greene quoted here in Babits and Howard, *Long, Obstinate, and Bloody*, 9–10.

167. Babits, *Devil of a Whipping*, 8–9.

168. Zambone, *Daniel Morgan*, 228–40.

169. Ibid., 241; Babits, *Devil of a Whipping*, 142; Morgan to Greene, January 19, 1781, *Greene Papers*, 7:152–54; Green to Washington, January 24, 1781, Founders Online, National Archives; Tarleton, *History of the Campaigns*, 260; Babits and Howard, *Long, Obstinate, and Bloody*, 13.

170. Cornwallis to Rawdon, January 21, 1781, *Cornwallis Papers*, 3:251.

171. Cornwallis to Clinton, January 6, 1781, *Cornwallis Papers*, 3:33–35; Saberton, *Cornwallis Papers*, 3:4, 12.

172. Cornwallis to Clinton, January 6, 1781, *Cornwallis Papers*, 3:33–35; Saberton, *Cornwallis Papers*, 3:4, 12.

173. Pension Application of William Neel, S15945, www.southerncampaign.org.

174. Cornwallis to Rawdon, January 25, 1781, *Cornwallis Papers*, 3:252; Saberton, *Cornwallis Papers*, 4:4; Cornwallis to Lord Germain, March 17, 1781, *Cornwallis Papers*, 4:12–13; Tarleton, *History of the Campaigns*, 223.

175. Babits and Howard, *Long, Obstinate, and Bloody*, 15–16.

176. Cornwallis to Lord Germain, March 17, 1781, *Cornwallis Papers*, 4:12–13; Lee, *Memoirs of the War*, 234; Pension Application of John Boyd, R1088, www.southerncampaign.org.

177. Morgan to Greene, January 25, 1781, *Greene Papers*, 7:201.

178. Greene to Isaac Huger, January 27, 1781, *Greene Papers*, 7:205; Greene to Samuel Huntington, January 31, 1781, *Greene Papers*, 7:225–26; Isaac Huger to Alexander Lillington, February 2, 1781, *Greene Papers*, 7:235; Lee, *Memoirs of the War*, 237.

179. Greene to William Campbell, January 30, 1781, *Greene Papers*, 7:218; Greene to Huger, January 30, 1781, *Greene Papers*, 7:219–20; Greene to the Officers Commanding the Militia in the Salisbury District, January 31, 1781, *Greene Papers*, 7:227–28.

180. Greene to Samuel Huntington, January 31, 1781, *Greene Papers*, 7:225–26; Greene to Colonel Hagens, January 31, 1781, *Cornwallis Papers*, 4:94.

181. Cornwallis to Lord Germain, March 17, 1781, *Cornwallis Papers*, 4:12–13; Carruthers, *Interesting Revolutionary Incidents and Sketches*, 403; Pension Application of John Hewitt, W2618, www.southerncampaign.org; Pension Application of Thomas Boyd, S17286, www.southerncampaign.org. Lieutenant Colonel Francis Hall of the Guards was also killed in this action while fording the river.

182. William Sharpe to George Washington, February 27, 1781, Founders Online, National Archives.

Chapter 9

183. Tarleton, *History of the Campaigns*, 225–26; Buchanan, *Road to Guilford Courthouse*, 344–48; Carruthers, *Interesting Revolutionary Incidents and Sketches*, 402; Pension Application of Elijah Dollar (Dollars), W17729, www.southerncampaign.org; Pension Application of Nathan Yarborough,

W4870, www.southerncampaign.org. The crossroads tavern, burned after the skirmish, was located at modern Mount Mourne at the intersection of Route 115 and Langtree Road, south of Mooresville.

184. Greene to Von Steuben, February 3, 1781, *Greene Papers*, 7:244n; Greene to George Washington, February 9, 1781, *Greene Papers*, 7:267; Pension Application of John Tuttle, W4836, www.southerncampaign.org.

185. Babits and Howard, *Long, Obstinate, and Bloody*, 26; Piecuch and Beakes, *"Light Horse Harry" Lee*, 96; "The Journal of the Honorable von Bose," typescript, S45, file A36, Guilford Courthouse National Military Park; Pension Application of James Conner, S8237, www.southerncampaign.org; Pension Application of John Boyd, R1088, www.southerncampaign.org.

186. Greene to Von Steuben, February 3, 1781, *Greene Papers*, 7:242–44; Piecuch and Beakes, *"Light Horse Harry" Lee*, 96–97. Greene was recalling Shakespeare's *Henry V*, Act 4, Scene 3, in which Westmoreland exclaims, "O that we now had here but one ten thousand of those men in England that do no work to-day!"

187. Babits and Howard, *Long, Obstinate, and Bloody*, 29; "Proceedings of a Council of War," February 9, 1781, *Greene Papers*, 7:261–62; Lee, *Memoirs of the War*, 236.

188. Cornwallis to Lord Rawdon, February 4, 1781, *Cornwallis Papers*, 4:44–45.

189. Urwin, "To Bring the American Army Under Strict Discipline," 4–26.

190. Pension Application of Francis Ketner, W20322, www.southerncampaign.org.

191. Lee, *Memoirs of the War*, 236; Greene to Abner Nash, February 9, 1781, *Greene's Papers*, 265n; Buchanan, *Road to Guilford Courthouse*, 354; Piecuch and Beakes, *"Cool Deliberate Courage,"* 75; Tarleton, *History of the Campaigns*, 228; Carruthers, *Interesting Revolutionary Incidents and Sketches*, 412.

192. Greene to Nash, February 9, 1781, *Greene Papers*, 7:263; Greene to Sumpter, February 9, 1781, *Greene Papers*, 7:266; "Proceedings of a Council of War," February 9, 1781, *Greene Papers*, 7:261–62; Lee, *Memoirs of the War*, 223; Massey and Piecuch, *General Nathanael Greene*, 9.

193. Greene to Washington, February 9, 1781, *Greene Papers*, 7:267–69.

194. Massey and Piecuch, *General Nathanael Greene*, 20.

195. Babits and Howard, *Long, Obstinate, and Bloody*, 30; Buchanan, *Road to Guilford Courthouse*, 355; Otho Williams to Greene, February 13, 1781, *Greene Papers*, 7:287n. The location of Dix's Ferry is incorrectly shown on map in *Greene Papers*, 7:213, and endpapers.

196. Otho Williams to Greene, February 11, 1781, *Greene Papers*, 7:282n; Greene to Williams, February 13, 1781, *Greene Papers*, 74:285; Lee, *Memoirs of the War*, 236–37.

197. Lee, *Memoirs of the War*, 238; Otho Williams to Greene, February 13, 1781, *Greene Papers*, 7:285; Tarleton, *History of the Campaigns*, 229.

198. Pension Application of John Hewitt, W2618, www.southerncampaign. org.

199. Aaron, *Race to the Dan*, 121.

200. Otho Williams to Greene, February 13, 1781, *Greene Papers*, 7:286; Lee, *Memoirs of the War*, 245; Greene to Washington, February 15, 1781, *Greene Papers*, 7:293; Newsome, "British Orderly Book," 367.

201. Lee, *Memoirs of the War*, 245–47; Aaron, *Race to the Dan*, 33; Greene to Otho Williams, February 14, 1781 (3 letters), *Greene Papers*, 287; Tarleton, *History of the Campaigns*, 229; Aaron, *Race to the Dan*, 121; Massey and Piecuch, *General Nathanael Greene*, 90. Lee stated that the army crossed on February 13, but Greene's letters show it was the fourteenth. Historians, writers, and even some participants have mischaracterized the retreat to the Dan as an event closely watched with anxiety by Americans at the time of the "race." In truth, the military maneuvers from the Catawba to the Dan, though dramatic, took just over two weeks; given the lack of newspapers and poor roads in the South, in addition to slow communications of the Revolutionary period, the vast majority of the public knew nothing of these events until long after the campaign was over.

202. Tarleton, *History of the Campaigns*, 229.

203. Massey and Piecuch, *General Nathanael Greene*, 19.

Chapter 10

204. Cornwallis to Germain, March 17, 1781, *Cornwallis Papers*, 4:13.

205. Ibid.

206. Ibid., 4:13–14.

207. Ibid., 4:14–15.

208. Ibid., 4:15; Red House Church was near the modern community of Sedalia, in Caswell County, North Carolina. Since 1913, a brick Neoclassical Revival church has occupied the site.

209. Pension Application of James Irvine, S4422, www.southerncampaign. org.

210. Newsome, "British Orderly Book," 371.

211. Cornwallis to Germain, March 17, 1781, *Cornwallis Papers*, 4:15; Proclamation, February 20, 1781, *Cornwallis Papers*, 4:55; "The Journal of the Honourable Regiment von Bose," typescript, S46, Guilford Courthouse National Military Park files, Box A36; Cornwallis to Benedict Arnold, February 21, 1781, *Cornwallis Papers*, 4:21; Carruthers, *Interesting Revolutionary Incidents and Sketches*, 416–18; Newsome, "British Orderly Book," 372.

212. Cornwallis to James Craig, February 21, 1781, *Cornwallis Papers*, 4:25; Charles Magill to Jefferson, March 2, 1781, *Jefferson Papers*, 5:43–45; Cornwallis to Nesbit Balfour, February 21, 1781, *Cornwallis Papers*, 4:41. Cross Creek was at modern Fayetteville.

213. Greene to Jefferson, February 15, 1781, *Greene Papers*, 7:289–90; Greene to North Carolina legislature, February 15, 1781, *Greene Papers*, 7:290–91; Greene to Von Steuben, February 15, 1781, *Greene Papers*, 7:292; Greene to John Butler, February 17, 1781, *Greene Papers*, 7:299; Pension Application of William Lesley, Guilford Courthouse National Military Park files.

214. Greene to Andrew Pickens, February 19, 1781, *Greene Papers*, 7:316.

215. Greene to Jefferson, March 10, 1781, *Greene Papers*, 7:419–20; Pension Application of William Lesley, Guilford Courthouse National Military Park files.

216. Greene to Andrew Pickens, February 19, 1781, *Greene Papers*, 7:316; Carruthers, *Interesting Revolutionary Incidents and Sketches*, 418; Newsome, "British Orderly Book," 373.

217. William Pierce Jr. to Robert Lawson, February 22, 1781, *Greene's Papers*, 7:332; Greene to Alexander Martin, February 19, 1781, *Greene's Papers*, 7:335; Massey and Piecuch, *General Nathanael Greene*, 13.

218. Pension Application of William Bowden, National Archives Microseries M804, Roll 298, no. S2388, www.southerncampaign.org.

219. Greene to John Butler, February 25, 1781, *Greene's Papers*, 7:347. High Rock Ford was on the Haw River where modern High Rock Road (Route 2620) crosses the river, one half mile south of Highrock Grove Baptist Church.

220. Maass, "Complicated Scene of Difficulties," 167, 182, 185, 457; Piecuch and Beakes, *"Light Horse Harry" Lee*, 106–7.

221. Lee to Greene, February 23, 1781, *Greene Papers*, 7:336; Babits and Howard, *Long, Obstinate, and Bloody*, 38–9; Piecuch and Beakes, *"Light Horse Harry" Lee*, 110–22; Cornwallis to Germain, March 17, 1781, *Cornwallis Papers*, 4:15; Dann, *Revolution Remembered*, 202. The approximate site of the action is near the intersection of Anthony Road and Old Trail Road, about two miles east of Alamance.

222. Carruthers, *Interesting Revolutionary Incidents and Sketches*, 425; Newsome, "British Orderly Book," 378–80.

223. Pension Application of Phillip Russell, W2575, www.southerncampaign.org.

224. The site of the skirmish is now covered by Lake Mackintosh, along Huffman Mill Road, southwest of Burlington.

225. Konstam, *Guilford Courthouse 1781*, 49–53; Piecuch and Beakes, *"Light Horse Harry" Lee*, 126–27; Murphy, *William Washington*, 101–3; Pension Application of Robert Love, S8858, www.southerncampaign.org. The mill site is on State Route 61, in Guilford County six miles north of Gibsonville.

226. Greene to Washington, February 28, 1781, *Greene Papers*, 7:370.

227. Piecuch and Beakes, *"Light Horse Harry" Lee*, 123; Andrew Pickens to Greene, February 26, 1781, *Greene Papers*, 7:358; Saberton, *Cornwallis Papers*, 4:6; Pension Application of William Lorance (Lowrance), S31217, www.southerncampaign.org; Magill to Jefferson, *Jefferson Papers*, 5:43–45.

228. Babits and Howard, *Long, Obstinate, and Bloody*, 44–47; Pickens to Greene, March 5, 1781, *Greene Papers*, 7:400n; Magill to Jefferson, March 10, 1781, *Jefferson Papers*, 5:115–16; Pension Application of Thomas Lovelady, W8065, www.southerncampaign.org.

229. Piecuch and Beakes, *"Light Horse Harry" Lee*, 128; Cornwallis to Germain, March 17, 1781, *Cornwallis Papers*, 4:16; Tarleton, *History of the Campaigns*, 238–39.

230. Cornwallis to Germain, March 17, 1781, *Cornwallis Papers*, 4:17; Baker, *Another Such Victory*, v. Deep River Friends Meeting was situated near today's intersection of West Wendover Avenue and Penny Road, High Point.

Chapter 11

231. Nathaniel Pendleton to Marquis de Malmedy, March 8, 1781, *Greene Papers*, 7:410.

232. Greene to Henry Lee, March 9, 1781, *Greene Papers*, 7:415–16.

233. Magill to Jefferson, March 8, 1781, *Jefferson Papers*, 5:93–94.

234. Greene to Henry Lee, March 9, 1781, *Greene's Papers*, 7:415; Greene to Jefferson, March 10, 1781, *Greene Papers*, 7:420.

235. Nathaniel Pendleton to Robert Lawson, March 8, 1781, *Greene Papers*, 7:410n; Greene to Jefferson, March 10, 1781, *Greene Papers*, 7:421n; Greene to Samuel Huntington, March 16, 1781, *Greene Papers*, 7:433–35; Greene to Lee, March 9, 1781, *Greene Papers*, 7:415.

236. Babits and Howard, *Long, Obstinate, and Bloody*, 69–78, 220–21; Magill to Jefferson, March 5, 1781, *Jefferson Papers*, 5:62–63; Reverend James Madison to James Madison, March 9, 1781, Founders Online, National Archives. By this time, General Caswell no longer commanded the state's militia.

237. Von Steuben to Jefferson, May 28, 1781, Founders Online, National Archives; Babits and Howard, *Long, Obstinate, and Bloody*, 69–78.

238. Babits and Howard, *Long, Obstinate, and Bloody*, 69–78, 220–21; Greene to Samuel Huntington, March 16, 1781, *Greene Papers*, 7:433.

239. Greene to Huger, February 5, 1781, *Greene Papers*, 7:252; Greene to Thomas Jefferson, March 16, 1781, *Greene Papers*, 7:441; Magill to Jefferson, March 10, 1781, *Jefferson Papers*, 5:116–18; Tucker, "Southern Campaign," 39; Greene to Henry Lee, March 14, 1781, *Greene Papers*, 7:430; Babits and Howard, *Long, Obstinate, and Bloody*, 50; Cornwallis to Germain, March 17, 1781, *Cornwallis Papers*, 4:17; Pension Application of James Martin, National Archives Microseries M804, Roll 1640, no. W4728; Greene to Samuel Huntington, March 16, 1781, *Greene Papers*, 7:433. Greene's offensive thinking was a departure from two previous engagements in the South in which Gates had intended to take a position inviting the enemy to attack him near Camden and in which Morgan deployed defensively at Cowpens.

240. Murphy, *William Washington*, 105; Pension Application of William Lorance (Lowrance), S31217, www.southerncampaign.org.

241. Greene to Lee, March 14, 1781, *Greene Papers*, 7:430; Greene to Samuel Huntington, March 16, 1781, *Greene Papers*, 7:433–35.

242. Pension Application of Benjamin Taylor, R10407, www. southerncampaign.org.

243. Cornwallis to Germain, 2 letters, March 17, 1781, *Cornwallis Papers*, 4:16, 17; Tarleton, *History of the Campaigns*, 270; von Bose diary, 48, transcription, Guilford Courthouse National Military Park, Greensboro.

244. Babits and Howard, *Long, Obstinate, and Bloody*, 50–51.

245. Tarleton, *History of the Campaigns*, 270–71; Lee, *Memoirs of the War*, 272–75; Babits and Howard, *Long, Obstinate, and Bloody*, 51–56; Hagist, *British Soldier's Story*, 84; see also Newlin, *Battle of New Garden*.

246. Morgan to Greene, February 20, 1781, *Greene Papers*, 7:324.

247. Pension Application of Nathan Slade, W6071, www.southerncampaign. org; Babits and Howard, *Long, Obstinate, and Bloody*, 59–65, 105.

248. Diary of Samuel Houston, in Foote, *Sketches of Virginia*, 141–49; Babits and Howard, *Long, Obstinate, and Bloody*, 65; Tarleton, *History of the Campaigns*, 271.

249. Babits and Howard, *Long, Obstinate, and Bloody*, 68–76.

250. Pension Application of Nathan Slade, W6071, www.southerncampaign.org.

251. Tarleton, *History of the Campaigns*, 271; Cornwallis to Germain, March 17, 1781, *Cornwallis Papers*, 17.

252. Babits and Howard, *Long, Obstinate, and Bloody*, 80–85, 105, 219–21; Saberton, "How Many Troops Did Cornwallis Actually Bring." Fortesque stated that the British had three cannons at their initial deployment, as does the map in Tarleton's memoirs (*War of Independence*, 226).

253. Tarleton, *History of the Campaigns*, 271.

Chapter 12

254. Babits and Howard, *Long, Obstinate, and Bloody*, 77–78; Piecuch and Beakes, *"Light Horse Harry" Lee*, 132; Pension Application of William Lesley, Guilford Courthouse National Military Park files; Pension Application of David Williams, S3578, www.southerncampaign.org.

255. Cornwallis to Germain, March 17, 1781, *Cornwallis Papers*, 17; Tarleton, *History of the Campaigns*, 272–73; Lee, *Memoirs of the War*, 276; Stedman, *History of the Origins, Progress, and Termination*, 2:383.

256. Greene to Samuel Huntington, March 16, 1781, *Greene Papers*, 7:434; Tarleton, *History of the Campaigns*, 272–73; Pension Application of James Hilton, National Archives Microseries M804, Roll 1282, no. S30484.

257. Cornwallis to Germain, March 17, 1781, *Cornwallis Papers*, 17–18; Tarleton, *History of the Campaigns*, 273; Babits and Howard, *Long, Obstinate, and Bloody*, 96, 101, 173, although the maps in the latter book incorrectly switch the positions of the two Guards battalions at initial deployment.

258. William Leslie Pension Application, Thomas Baker Collection, First Line primary accounts, Guilford Courthouse National Military Park Collection.

259. Pension Application of James Martin, National Archives Microseries M804, Roll 1640, no. W4728.

260. Stedman quoted in Hagist, *British Soldier's Story*, 85. Charles Stedman was a Philadelphia Loyalist who fled with the British when they evacuated the city in 1778. He became Cornwallis's commissary general in 1780, a civilian position, and witnessed the battle.

261. Tarleton, *History of the Campaigns*, 273.

262. Hagist, *British Soldier's Story*, 89.

263. Babits and Howard, *Long, Obstinate, and Bloody*, 101.

264. Stedman quoted in Hagist, *British Soldier's Story*, 85; Babits and Howard, *Long, Obstinate, and Bloody*, 100.

265. Pension Application of William Haynie, W7693, www.southerncampaign.org.

266. Hamilton, *Origin and History of the First of Grenadier Guards*, 2:248.

267. Babits and Howard, *Long, Obstinate, and Bloody*, 103, 108.

268. Otho H. Williams to Josias Carveill, March 17, 1781, Guilford Courthouse National Military Park files.

269. Pension Application of Henry Connelly, W8188, www.southerncampaign.org.

270. Greene to Samuel Huntington, March 16, 1781, *Greene Papers*, 7:434.

271. Greene to Jefferson, March 16, 1781, *Greene Papers*, 7:441.

272. Greene to Washington, March 18, 1781, *Greene Papers*, 7:451.

273. Greene to Thomas Sumter, March 16, 1781, *Greene Papers*, 7:442.

274. Greene to Abner Nash, March 18, 1781, *Greene Papers*, 7:448.

275. Greene to Joseph Read, March 18, 1781, *Greene Papers*, 7:450.

276. Lee, *Memoirs of the War*, 277–78.

277. Ibid., 278.

278. James Collins Sr. Pension Application, Baker Collection, First Line primary accounts, Guilford Courthouse National Military Park Collection.

279. Pension Application of Nathan Slade, W6071, www.southerncampaign.org.

280. Babits and Howard, *Long, Obstinate, and Bloody*, 64–65, 104; Lee, *Memoirs of the War*, 278–79; Cornwallis to Germain, March 17, 1781, *Cornwallis Papers*, 18; Tarleton, *History of the Campaigns*, 275, Cornwallis to Germain, March 17, 1781, *Cornwallis Papers*, 4:18. This fighting took place on the high ground in what is now Greensboro Country Park near Shelter 5.

281. Tarleton, *History of the Campaigns*, 275–76.

282. Ibid., 275–76; Babits and Howard, *Long, Obstinate, and Bloody*, 129; Pension Application of James Hilton, National Archives Microseries M804, Roll 1282, no. S30484.

283. Lee, *Memoirs of the War*, 281–83; Piecuch and Beakes, *"Light Horse Harry" Lee*, 134, 136–37; Pension Application of Joseph Marler, R6934, www.southerncampaigns.org; Buchanan, *Road to Guilford Courthouse*, 380; Massey and Piecuch, *General Nathanael Greene*, 94; Babits and Howard, *Long, Obstinate, and Bloody*, 138–39; Hagist, *British Soldier's Story*, 88; Pension Application of James Braden (Brady), R1124, www.southerncampaign.org.

284. Cornwallis to Germain, March 17, 1781, *Cornwallis Papers*, 4:18; Tarleton, *History of the Campaigns*, 274.

285. Murphy, *William Washington*, 108–10.

Chapter 13

286. Babits and Howard, *Long, Obstinate, and Bloody*, chapter 7.

287. Ibid., 117.

288. Hamilton, *Origin and History of the First of Grenadier Guards*, 2:248.

289. Tucker, "Southern Campaign," 40–42; Babits and Howard, *Long, Obstinate, and Bloody*, 119.

290. Babits and Howard, *Long, Obstinate, and Bloody*, 119.

291. Greene to Samuel Huntington, March 16, 1781, *Greene Papers*, 7:435.

292. Hagist, *British Soldier's Story*, 85; Hamilton, *Origin and History of the First of Grenadier Guards*, 2:248; Pension Application of James Johnston, VAS1258, www.southerncampaign.org.

293. Greene to Joseph Reid, March 18, 1781, *Greene Papers*, 7:450.

294. Greene to Washington, March 18, 1781, *Greene Papers*, 7:451; Otho H. Williams to Josias Carveill, March 17, 1781, Guilford Courthouse National Military Park files.

295. Babits and Howard, *Long, Obstinate, and Bloody*, 120.

296. Ibid.

297. Cornwallis to Germain, March 17, 1781, *Cornwallis Papers*, 4:18.

298. Babits and Howard, *Long, Obstinate, and Bloody*, 122.

299. Ibid.

300. Murphy, *William Washington*, 109; Pension Application of Richard Daniel, S8293, www.southerncampaign.org; Pension Application of Samuel Davison, R2694, www.southerncamp.org.

301. Babits and Howard, *Long, Obstinate, and Bloody*, 122–23.

302. Piecuch and Beakes, *"Cool Deliberate Courage,"* 89.

303. Cornwallis to Germain, March 17, 1781, *Cornwallis Papers*, 4:18.

304. Urban, *Fusiliers*, 243; Babits and Howard, *Long, Obstinate, and Bloody*, 126.

305. Pension Application of Lewis Griffin, S21248, www.southerncampaign.org.

306. "The 1781 Journal of Samuel Houston," Guilford Courthouse National Military Park files; Sanders, "Liberty, Liberty," 1–7; Diehl, "Rockbridge Men at War," 261–65; Samuel McDowell to Thomas Jefferson, April 20, 1781, Founders Online, National Archives.

307. Tucker, "Southern Campaign," 40–42; Pension Application of Joseph Dameron, S8310, and Pension Application of Thomas Kitchen (Kitchens), R5998, www.southerncampaign.org.

308. Tarleton, *History of the Campaigns*, 273–74.

309. Greene to Jefferson, March 16, 1781, *Greene Papers*, 7:441; Babits and Howard, *Long, Obstinate, and Bloody*, 142.

310. Babits and Howard, *Long, Obstinate, and Bloody*, 127.

Chapter 14

311. Tarleton, *History of the Campaigns*, 274; Piecuch and Beakes, *"Cool Deliberate Courage,"* 90.

312. Babits and Howard, *Long, Obstinate, and Bloody*, 143–44, 157; Hobson, *Papers of John Marshall*, 4:342–44.

313. Lee, *Memoirs of the War*, 279.

314. Ibid., 279; Piecuch and Beakes, *"Cool Deliberate Courage,"* 90; Pension Application of Lewis Griffin, S21248, www.southerncampaign.org.

315. Tarleton, *History of the Campaigns*, 274.

316. Babits and Howard, *Long, Obstinate, and Bloody*, 147; Hobson, *Papers of John Marshall*, 4:342–44.

317. Cornwallis to Germaine, March 17, 1781, *Cornwallis Papers*, 4:18; Greene to Samuel Huntington, March 16, 1781, *Greene Papers*, 7:440n.

318. Cornwallis to Germaine, March 17, 1781, *Cornwallis Papers*, 4:18; Greene to Samuel Huntington, March 16, 1781, *Greene Papers*, 7:440n.

319. Cornwallis to Germaine, March 17, 1781, *Cornwallis Papers*, 4:18; Hobson, *Papers of John Marshall*, 4:342–44.

320. Piecuch and Beakes, *"Cool Deliberate Courage,"* 90–91; O'Donnell, *Washington's Immortals*, 321; Hobson, *Papers of John Marshall*, 4:342–44.

321. Hobson, *Papers of John Marshall*, 4:342–44.

322. Tarleton, *History of the Campaigns*, 275; Greene to Samuel Huntington, March 16, 1781, *Greene Papers*, 7:440n, 114.

323. Murphy, *William Washington*, 115.

324. Babits and Howard, *Long, Obstinate, and Bloody*, 160; Pension Application of Peter Francisco, W11021, www.southerncampaign.org.

325. O'Donnell, *Washington's Immortals*, 321.

326. Hobson, *Papers of John Marshall*, 4:342–44; Piecuch and Beakes, *"Cool Deliberate Courage,"* 91.

327. Piecuch and Beakes, *"Cool Deliberate Courage,"* 91.

328. Babits and Howard, *Long, Obstinate, and Bloody*, 161–63; Piecuch and Beakes, *"Cool Deliberate Courage,"* 91.

329. Piecuch and Beakes, *"Cool Deliberate Courage,"* 91; Hobson, *Papers of John Marshall*, 4:342–44.

330. Greene to Catherine Greene, March 18, 1781, *Greene Papers*, 7:446–47n.

331. Lee, *Memoirs of the War*, 281.

332. Babits and Howard, *Long, Obstinate, and Bloody*, 164; Piecuch and Beakes, "*Cool Deliberate Courage*," 92; Hobson, *Papers of John Marshall*, 4:342–44.

333. Pension Application of Lewis Griffin, S21248, www.southerncampaign.org.

334. Tarleton, *History of the Campaigns*, 276; Greene to Daniel Morgan, March 20, 1781, *Greene Papers*, 7:455–56n; Babits and Howard, *Long, Obstinate, and Bloody*, 166–67; Magill to Jefferson, March 16, 1781, *Papers of Thomas Jefferson*, 5:162–63; Pension Application of James Cotton, National Archives Microseries M804, Roll 661, no. W6942, www.southerncampaign.org.

335. Cornwallis to Germain, March 17, 1781, *Cornwallis Papers*, 4:19; Babits and Howard, *Long, Obstinate, and Bloody*, 173; Lee, *Memoirs of the War*, 284, 286; Newsome, "British Orderly Book," 388.

336. Babits and Howard, *Long, Obstinate, and Bloody*, 175; Greene to Samuel Huntington, March 16, 1781, *Greene Papers*, 7:435.

337. Greene to Joseph Reid, March 18, 1781, *Greene Papers*, 7:450.

338. Abraham Clark to Elias Dayton, April 1, 1781, Smith, *Letters of Delegates*, 17:111.

339. Lee, *Memoirs of the War*, 286.

340. Pension Application of Peter Lesley, National Archives Microseries M804, Roll 1551, no. S4540; Pension Application of Thomas Green, S31702, www.southerncampaign.org; Pension Application of Benedict Wadkins, W11709, www.southerncampaign.org.

341. Tucker, "Southern Campaign," 40–42; Otho H. Williams to Josias Carveill, March 17, 1781, Guilford Courthouse National Military Park files; Lee, *Memoirs of the War*, 286.

342. Storozynski, *Peasant Prince*, 99; Stedman, *History of the Origins, Progress, and Termination*, 2:382; Ketchum, "England's Vietnam"; Clinton, *Observations on Mr. Stedman's* History of the American War, 17.

343. Greene to Abner Nash, March 18, 1781, *Greene Papers*, 7:448; Greene to Joseph Reid, March 18, 1781, *Greene Papers*, 7:451; Greene to Benjamin Cleveland, March 19, 1781, *Greene Papers*, 7:453.

Chapter 15

344. "Summons to Arms," March 17, 1781, *Cornwallis Papers*, 4:57–58.

345. "Proclamation," March 18, 1781, *Cornwallis Papers*, 4:58.

346. Newsome, "British Orderly Book," 389.

347. Tarleton, *History of the Campaigns*, 279; Cornwallis to Clinton, April 10, 1781, *Cornwallis Papers*, 4:110.

348. Greene to Catherine Greene, March 18, 1781, *Greene Papers*, 7:446; Greene to Washington, March 18, 1781, *Greene Papers*, 7:452.

349. Tarleton, *History of the Campaigns*, 280, 322; Greene to Lee, March 22, 1781, *Greene Papers*, 7:461; Buchanan, *Road to Charleston*, 65.

350. Tarleton, *History of the Campaigns*, 321; Greene to Samuel Huntington, March 23, 1781, *Greene Papers*, 7:464; Greene to Jefferson, March 27, 1781, *Greene Papers*, 7:471; Abner Nash to Washington, April 4, 1781, Founders Online, National Archives.

351. Pension Application of Thomas Cook, S31618, and Nathaniel Dacus, S21153, www.southerncampaign.org.

352. Pension Application of Benjamin Copeland, S21122, and Lewis Griffin, S21248, www.southerncampaign.org.

353. Pension Application of James Cotton, National Archives Microseries M804, Roll 661, no. W6942.

354. Tarleton, *History of the Campaigns*, 280, 322; Greene to Lee, March 22, 1781, *Greene Papers*, 7:461; Buchanan, *Road to Charleston*, 65.

355. Greene to Marquis de Lafayette, March 29, 1781, *Greene Papers*, 7:478; Greene to Washington, March 29, 1781, *Greene Papers*, 7:481.

356. Greene to Washington, March 29, 1781, *Greene Papers*, 7:481–82; Greene to James Emmett, April 3, 1781, *Greene Papers*, 8:481; Buchanan, *Road to Charleston*, 39, 47.

357. Cornwallis to Clinton, April 10, 1781, *CSRNC*, 17:1,010–12.

358. Of note, although Greene severely and repeatedly criticized the North Carolina militia for fleeing the first line, he said little about the 2nd Maryland doing the same thing on the third line.

359. Massey and Piecuch, *General Nathanael Greene*, 8.

360. Greene to Alexander Lillington, March 29, 1781, *Greene Papers*, 7:479.

BIBLIOGRAPHY

Aaron, Larry G. *The Race to the Dan.* Halifax, VA: Halifax County Historical Society, 2007.

Anderson, Eric. "William Washington." *On Point* 20 (2015): 18–21.

Babits, Lawrence E. *A Devil of a Whipping: The Battle of Cowpens.* Chapel Hill: University of North Carolina Press, 1988.

Babits, Lawrence E., and Joshua L. Howard. *Long, Obstinate, and Bloody: The Battle of Guilford Courthouse.* Chapel Hill: University of North Carolina Press, 2013.

Baker, Thomas E. *Another Such Victory.* Fort Washington, PA: Eastern National, 1981.

Billias, George A., ed. *George Washington's Generals.* New York: William Morrow and Company, 1944.

———. *George Washington's Generals and Opponents: Their Exploits and Leadership.* New York: Da Capo Press, 1994.

Boatner, Mark M., III. *Encyclopedia of the American Revolution.* Reprint, Mechanicsburg, PA: Stackpole Books, 1994.

Borick, Carl P. *A Gallant Defense: The Siege of Charleston.* Columbia: University of South Carolina Press, 2003.

Boyd, Julian, et al., eds. *The Papers of Thomas Jefferson.* Princeton, NJ: Princeton University Press, 1950–.

Buchanan, John. *The Road to Charleston: Nathanael Greene and the American Revolution.* Charlottesville: University of Virginia Press, 2019.

———. *The Road to Guilford Courthouse: The American Revolution in the Carolinas.* New York: Wiley & Sons, 1999.

Carbone, Gerald. *Nathanael Greene: A Biography of the American Revolution.* New York: St. Martin's, 2010.

Carruthers, Eli W. *Interesting Revolutionary Incidents and Sketches of Characters Chiefly in the Old North State.* Philadelphia, PA: Hayes and Zell, 1856.

Clark, Walter, ed. *The Colonial and State Records of North Carolina.* 26 vols. Goldsboro, NC: Nash Brothers, 1886–1907.

Clinton, Henry. *Observations on Mr. Stedman's* History of the American War. London, 1794.

Dann, John C., ed. *The Revolution Remembered: Eyewitness Accounts of the War for Independence.* Chicago: University of Chicago Press, 1980.

Diehl, George. "Rockbridge Men at War." *Daughters of the American Revolution Magazine* (March 1968): 261–65.

Draper, Lyman C. *King's Mountain and Its Heroes.* Cincinnati, OH: P.G. Thompson, 1881.

Foote, William Henry. *Sketches of Virginia: Historical and Biographical.* Philadelphia, PA: J.B. Lippincott & Company, Philadelphia, 1855.

Fortesque, John. *The War of Independence: The British Army in North America, 1775–1783.* London: Greenhill Books, 2001.

Founders Online. National Archives. http://founders.archives.gov.

Golway, Terry. *Washington's General: Nathanael Greene and the Triumph of the American Revolution.* New York: Henry Holt, 2005.

Hagist, Don N., ed. *A British Soldier's Story: Roger Lamb's Narrative of the American Revolution.* Baraboo, WI: Ballindoch Press, 2004.

Hamilton, F.W. *The Origin and History of the First of Grenadier Guards.* 3 vols. London: John Murray, 1874.

Higgins, W. Robert, ed. *The Revolutionary War in the South: Power, Conflict, and Leadership.* Durham, NC: Duke University Press, 1979.

Hobson, Charles F., ed. *The Papers of John Marshall.* 12 vols. Chapel Hill: University of North Carolina, 2012.

Ketchum, Richard. "England's Vietnam: The American Revolution." *American Heritage* 22 (1971). https://www.americanheritage.com/englands-vietnam-american-revolution.

Konstam, Angus. *Guilford Courthouse 1781: Lord Cornwallis's Ruinous Victory.* Oxford, UK: Osprey, 2002.

Lathan, Robert S. "We Are Family." *Davidson Journal,* July 29, 2002. http://davidsonjournal.davidson.edu/2012/07/we-are-family.

Lee, Henry. *Memoirs of the War in the Southern Department of the United States*. Rev. ed. New York: University Publishing Company, 1869.

Lee, Wayne E. *Crowds and Soldiers in Revolutionary War North Carolina: The Culture of Violence in Riot and War*. Gainesville: University Press of Florida, 2001.

Lefler, Hugh T., and Albert R. Newsome. *North Carolina: The History of a Southern State*. Chapel Hill: University of North Carolina Press, 1954.

Lengel, Edward G. *General George Washington: A Military Life*. New York: Random House, 2005.

Lynch, Wayne. "Winner or Runner?" *Journal of the American Revolution* (April 8, 2014). Accessed at All Things Liberty. https://allthingsliberty. com/2014/04/winner-or-runner-gates-at-camden/#edn5.

Maass, John R. "'A Complicated Scene of Difficulties': North Carolina and the Revolutionary Settlement, 1776–1789." Diss., Ohio State University, 2007.

———. *Horatio Gates and the Battle of Camden—"That Unhappy Affair," August 16, 1780*. Camden, SC: Kershaw County Historical Society, 2001.

———. *The Road to Yorktown: Jefferson, Lafayette and the British Invasion of Virginia*. Charleston, SC: The History Press, 2015.

Martin, James Kirby, and David L. Preston, eds. *Theaters of the American Revolution*. Yardley, PA: Westholme, 2017.

Massey, Gregory D., and Jim Piecuch, eds. *General Nathanael Greene and the American Revolution in the South*. Columbia: University of South Carolina Press, 2012.

Morgan, Curtis F., Jr. "Nathanael Greene as Quartermaster General." *Journal of the American Revolution* (November 18, 2013). Accessed at All Things Liberty. https://allthingsliberty.com/2013/11/nathanael-greene-quartermaster-general/#comment-121652.

Murphy, Daniel. *William Washington: An American Light Dragoon*. Yardley, PA: Westholme Publishing, 2014.

Newlin, Algie. *The Battle of New Garden*. Greensboro: North Carolina Friends Historical Society, 1995.

Newsome, A.R. "A British Orderly Book, 1780–1781, IV." *North Carolina Historical Review* 9 (1932).

O'Donnell, Patrick K. *Washington's Immortals*. New York: Atlantic Monthly Press, 2016.

O'Shaughnessy, Andrew J. *The Men Who Lost America: British Leadership, the American Revolution, and the Fate of the Empire*. New Haven, CT: Yale University Press, 2013.

Pancake, John. *This Destructive War: The British Campaign in the Carolinas, 1780–1782*. Tuscaloosa: University of Alabama Press, 1985.

The Papers of Alexander Hamilton. 27 vols. New York: Columbia University Press, 1962–87.

Patten, David. "Ferguson and His Rifle." *History Today* 28 (1978).

Piecuch, Jim. *The Battle of Camden: A Documentary History*. Charleston, SC: The History Press, 2006.

———. *Three Peoples, One King: Loyalists, Indians, and Slaves in the American Revolutionary South, 1775–1782*. Columbia: University of South Carolina Press, 2008.

Piecuch, Jim, and John Beakes. *"Cool Deliberate Courage": John Eager Howard in the American Revolution*. Charleston, SC: Naval and Aviation Publishing Company, 2009.

———. *"Light Horse Harry" Lee in the War for Independence*. Charleston, SC: Nautical and Aviation Publishing Company, 2013.

Rauch, Steven J. "Southern Discomfort: British Phase IV Operations in South Carolina and Georgia, May–September 1780." *Army History* 71 (2009): 34–50.

Robinson, Blackwell P. *Revolutionary War Sketches of William R. Davie*. Raleigh: North Carolina Department of Cultural Resources, Division of Archives and History, 1976.

———. *William R. Davie*. Chapel Hill: University of North Carolina Press, 1957.

Saberton, Ian. "Cornwallis and the Autumn Campaign of 1780—His Advance from Camden to Charlotte." *Journal of the American Revolution* (July 18, 2017). Accessed at All Things Liberty. https://allthingsliberty.com/2017/07/cornwallis-autumn-campaign-1780-advance-camden-charlotte.

———. "How Many Troops Did Cornwallis Actually Bring to the Battle of Guilford?" *Journal of the American Revolution* (May 10, 2017). Accessed at All Things Liberty. https://allthingsliberty.com/2017/05/many-troops-cornwallis-actually-bring-battle-guilford.

Saberton, Ian, ed. *The Cornwallis Papers: The Campaigns of 1780 and 1781 in the Southern Theatre of the American Revolutionary War*. 6 vols. Sussex, England, UK: Naval and Military Press, 2010.

Sanders, I. Taylor. "Liberty, Liberty: The Academy and the Revolution." *Washington and Lee University Alumni Magazine* 51, no. 8 (n.d.): 1–7.

Scheer, George F., and Hugh F. Rankin. *Rebels and Redcoats: The American Revolution through the Eyes of Those Who Fought and Lived It*. Reprint, New York: Da Capo Press, 1987.

Schellhammer, Michael. "Tarleton: Before He Became 'Bloody Ban.'" *Journal of the American Revolution* (January 29, 2013). Accessed at All Things Liberty. https://allthingsliberty.com/2013/01/tarleton-in-new-york.

Scoggins, Michael. *The Day It Rained Militia: Huck's Defeat and the Revolution in the South Carolina Backcountry*. Charleston, SC: The History Press, 2005.

Scotti, Anthony J., Jr. *Brutal Virtue: The Myth and Reality of Banastre Tarleton*. Bowie, MD: Heritage Books, 2002.

Seymour, William. "Journal of the Southern Expedition, 1780–1783." *Pennsylvania Magazine of History and Biography* 7 (1883): 286–98, 377–94.

Shachtman, Tom. *How the French Saved America*. New York: St. Martin's Press, 2017.

Showman, Richard K., Dennis M. Conrad et al., eds. *The Papers of General Nathanael Greene*. 13 vols. Chapel Hill: University of North Carolina Press, 1976–2005.

Smith, David. *Camden 1780: The Annihilation of Gates' Grand Army*. Oxford, UK: Osprey, 2016.

Smith, Paul H., ed. *Letters of Delegates to Congress*. 26 vols. Washington, D.C.: Library of Congress, 1976–2000.

Stedman, Charles. *The History of the Origins, Progress, and Termination of the American War*. 2 vols. London: J. Murray, 1794.

Stevens, Benjamin F. *The Campaign in Virginia, 1781: An Exact Reprint of Six Rare Pamphlets on the Clinton-Cornwallis Controversy*. 2 vols. London: self-published, 1888.

Stevens, John A. "The Southern Campaign." *Magazine of American History* 5 (1880).

Storozynski, Alex. *The Peasant Prince: Thaddeus Kosciuszko and the Age of Revolution*. New York: St. Martins, 2009.

Taffee, Stephen R. *The Philadelphia Campaign, 1777–1778*. Lawrence: University Press of Kansas, 2003.

Tarleton, Banastre. *A History of the Campaigns of 1780 and 1781 in the Southern Provinces of North America*. Reprint, New York: Ayer Publishing, 1968.

Tucker, Spencer. *Rise and Fight Again: The Life of Nathanael Greene*. Wilmington, DE: ISI Books, 2009.

Tucker, St. George. "The Southern Campaign, 1781: From Guilford Courthouse to the Siege of York...." *Magazine of American History* 7 (1881).

Urban, Mark. *Fusiliers: The Saga of a British Redcoat Regiment in the American Revolution*. New York: Walker Books, 2007.

Urwin, Gregory. "'To Bring the American Army Under Strict Discipline': British Army Foraging Policy in the South, 1780–81." *War in History* 26 (2019): 4–26.

Weddle, Kevin J. "'A Change of Both Men and Measures': British Reassessment of Military Strategy After Saratoga, 1777–1778." *Journal of Military History* 77 (2013): 837–65.

Willcox, William B. *Portrait of a General: Sir Henry Clinton in the War for Independence.* New York: Knopf, 1964.

Wilson, David K. *The Southern Strategy: Britain's Conquest of South Carolina and Georgia, 1775–1780.* Columbia: University of South Carolina Press, 2008.

Zambone, Albert L. *Daniel Morgan: A Revolutionary Life.* Yardley, PA: Westholme Publishing, 2018.

INDEX

About the Author

B orn on Long Island, New York, and raised in Rockbridge County, Virginia, John R. Maass is an education staff member of the new National Museum of the U.S. Army at Fort Belvoir. Previously, he was a historian at the U.S. Army Center of Military History in Washington, D.C., for ten years. Dr. Maass received a BA in history from Washington and Lee University (magna cum laude), an MA in American history from University of North Carolina–Greensboro, and a PhD in early American history at the Ohio State University. He is the author of several books and numerous articles on early U.S. military history, including *North Carolina and the French and Indian War: The Spreading Flames of War* (2013); *Defending a New Nation, 1783–1811* (2013); *The Road to Yorktown: Jefferson, Lafayette and the British Invasion of Virginia* (2015); and *George Washington's Virginia* (2017). Dr. Maass was an officer in the U.S. Army Reserves, founder of the Rockbridge Civil War Round Table, and recipient of the first Tyree-Lamb Fellowship from the Society of the Cincinnati. A frequent speaker on historical topics and a Revolutionary War battlefield tour guide, he is currently coauthoring a book on the military history of North Carolina.

Visit us at
www.historypress.com